CW00688661

CSIRO is Australia's national science agency and one of the largest and most diverse research agencies in the world. We're solving Australia's biggest health and biosecurity challenges through innovative science and technology. With decades of experience in delivering ground-breaking health initiatives, we're partnering with our nation's food, health and wellness industries to deliver health solutions to benefit all Australians.

# The CSIRO LOW-CARB DIET
# QUICK & EASY

PROFESSOR GRANT BRINKWORTH
AND DR PENNIE TAYLOR

Pan Macmillan Australia

# Contents

# About the authors

### PROFESSOR GRANT BRINKWORTH

Grant is a senior principal research scientist at CSIRO Health and Biosecurity. He has a PhD and expertise in diet, nutrition and exercise science. Grant has more than 18 years' experience leading large-scale, multidisciplinary clinical research teams and studies evaluating the effects of dietary patterns, foods, nutritional components and physical exercise on weight loss, metabolic disease risk management, health and performance in healthy and clinical populations.

Grant has particular interests in developing effective lifestyle and technology solutions for achieving optimal weight, metabolic health and diabetes management, and understanding the role of lower-carbohydrate dietary patterns for health and disease-risk management. He has published more than 100 peer-reviewed scientific papers on the topic of diet and lifestyle management of obesity and related diseases. Grant is the co-author of the number-one bestselling book *The CSIRO Low-Carb Diet*, as well as the bestselling *CSIRO Low-Carb Every Day* and *CSIRO Protein Plus*. He also holds a Masters of Business Administration degree with a focus on innovation and the commercialisation of science outcomes and lifestyle programs for large-scale community adoption and impact.

## DR PENNIE TAYLOR

Pennie is a senior dietitian and research scientist in the Nutrition and Health program at CSIRO Health and Biosecurity. She has completed her PhD at the University of Adelaide, School of Medicine, in dietary factors and the integrated role of emerging health technologies including Real Time Continuous Glucose Monitoring for health and type 2 diabetes management.

Pennie holds a master's degree in Nutrition and Dietetics at Flinders University and has extensive clinical expertise, including diet design for complex clinical trials and the development of community weight management and chronic disease programs specialising in obesity, diabetes, cardiovascular diseases and weight-loss surgery. She is the co-author of the number-one bestselling book *The CSIRO Low-Carb Diet*, as well as the bestselling *CSIRO Low-Carb Every Day*. Pennie works closely with industry partners to adapt science into clinical and community outcomes and has an interest in strategies to optimise glucose control, appetite response and eating behaviours for improved health and wellbeing. She also practises privately at EvolvME to maintain a close understanding of new innovations in the health environment and consumer health needs, which she has done for over 15 years.

# Introduction

The CSIRO's health and nutrition laboratories have long been at the forefront of nutrition research, involved in many experimental activities and clinical trials to identify dietary patterns and nutritional and lifestyle strategies that support weight loss and overall health.

While nutrition science is constantly evolving, the CSIRO has gained an international reputation as leaders in the field, offering trusted, scientifically based diet, exercise and lifestyle solutions that have helped hundreds of thousands of Australians better manage their weight and improve their health and wellbeing.

## THE LOW-CARB JOURNEY

For many years, the CSIRO has been researching the health effects of low-carb, higher protein and healthy fat diets, and has demonstrated how effective these are not only for weight loss and long-term weight management, but also for normalising blood-glucose levels and improving metabolic health in those with conditions such as type 2 diabetes, insulin resistance and metabolic syndrome.

In 2017, *The CSIRO Low-Carb Diet* was published in Australia, detailing a scientifically proven dietary and lifestyle plan for effectively promoting substantial weight loss and improving health and wellbeing. This ground-breaking book became a number one bestseller, selling over 100,000 copies and helping countless Australians to achieve significant health benefits.

So great was the interest in the program, from both the public as well as doctors and other health practitioners, that a companion book, *CSIRO Low-Carb Every Day*, was released in 2018, providing complementary recipes, meal builders and exercise options to make it even easier to adopt the program as a regular part of everyday life. This book, too, became a top ten bestseller, selling over 50,000 copies.

In Australia today, two in three adults are overweight or obese. The growing prevalence of obesity – along with the rise in chronic diseases such as heart disease and type 2 diabetes, which are closely underpinned by dietary and lifestyle factors – is driving many Australians to seek out credible information and diet and lifestyle solutions that are safe, effective and achievable.

*The popularity of these books is largely due to the strong scientific evidence supporting the CSIRO Low-Carb Diet and lifestyle plan, including the rigorous clinical research conducted by the CSIRO and other leading scientific institutions around the world.*

ASSOC. PROF. GRANT BRINKWORTH AND PENNIE TAYLOR

PROFESSOR GRANT BRINKWORTH AND PENNIE TAYLOR

## NOT JUST A PASSING FAD

Our passion at the CSIRO is not only to develop dietary strategies that will help people lose weight – since any diet that gets you to eat less will do that – but to use the latest nutrition knowledge and proven scientific principles to help people achieve their long-term weight management goals, while at the same time maximising improvements in overall health.

While the concept of 'low carb' eating has been around for many years, it has recently become hugely popular, largely because of our deeper understanding about how various dietary factors affect our health and wellbeing, and the enormous health benefits that can be achieved by adopting a lower-carb diet – especially for those who may have gained only modest improvements and benefits from traditional dietary approaches.

In fact, rigorous research has demonstrated that, compared to a traditional high-unrefined-carbohydrate, low-fat diet, the CSIRO Low-Carb Diet – which is much lower in carbohydrate, and proportionally higher in protein and unsaturated 'healthy' fats – is not only effective in promoting substantial weight loss, but delivers greater improvements in blood-glucose control and normalising blood-cholesterol levels.

This is particularly beneficial for the management of conditions such as insulin resistance, metabolic syndrome, pre-diabetes and type 2 diabetes, which are affecting more and more of our population.

Our research has also shown that this eating and lifestyle plan and its related health improvements are sustainable over the long term, and are not just a short-lived fad – another reason why so many people have embraced it.

## MAKING LOW-CARB EATING EVEN EASIER

At the CSIRO we are always looking for ways to make healthy and effective choices the easy choice, so in response to reader demand we are pleased to present *The CSIRO Low-Carb Diet Quick & Easy*, offering another comprehensive selection of satisfying and delicious recipes to complement the CSIRO Low-Carb Diet plan.

Very importantly, besides being tasty and nutritious, all the recipes in this book are very fast and simple to prepare – most of them have fewer than 10 ingredients, and all of them are cooked in 20 minutes or less – to make healthy eating even easier to manage within the busiest of lifestyles.

In this book, as well as offering two Q&A sections summarising some of the science behind the diet (including an update on the latest findings on low-carb dieting), and explaining how to best put it all into practice in your kitchen, we have also provided two simplified weekly menu plans, to show you how easy it is to make this dietary plan part of your everyday life.

We hope this book will make it even easier for you to adopt this eating philosophy and lifestyle over the long term, and enjoy the improved health and wellbeing that it can deliver.

### THE RECIPES IN THIS BOOK:

* are CSIRO low-carb friendly
* are cooked in 20 minutes or less
* are nutritious and, best of all, tasty!

PART 1

# THE CSIRO
## Low-Carb Diet

# THE SCIENCE:
## *An overview*

### *Q.* WHAT IS THE CSIRO LOW-CARB DIET?

*A.* With a strong focus on nutrient-dense whole foods, the CSIRO Low-Carb Diet is an evidence-based, nutritionally complete, energy-controlled plan that reduces the overall amount of carbohydrate consumed, while also increasing the level of healthy (unsaturated) fats and protein in the diet.

Research published in leading scientific journals by reputable scientific groups from around the world supports the effectiveness of this diet plan because it offers several important health benefits:

1. **It limits the consumption of high-carbohydrate foods, which helps control blood-glucose levels.** Eating higher amounts of high-carb foods such as breads, cereals, rice, pasta, potatoes and foods high in sugar can cause blood-glucose levels to rapidly rise, which can promote an increased risk of type 2 diabetes and heart disease, along with the health consequences associated with these conditions. Selecting low-glycaemic index (GI) options of these carbohydrate-rich foods can assist in lowering these post-eating blood glucose rises. However, reducing the amount of high-carb foods and the total amount of carbohydrate in the diet will have the greater impact in reducing the glycaemic load and our blood-glucose response after eating, making it easier to achieve more stable blood-glucose levels throughout the day, which is especially important in managing conditions such as insulin resistance and diabetes.

2. **It is rich in heart-healthy unsaturated fats.** Not all fats are equal, and unsaturated fats actually *improve* heart health. Unsaturated fats (which include monounsaturated and polyunsaturated fats) are naturally found in nuts, seeds, oils (olive, canola, sunflower and sesame), avocado, olives and oily fish such as salmon and tuna, all of which are generously included in the CSIRO Low-Carb Diet and help to further reduce the blood-glucose level rises when eaten with carbohydrate.

3. **It is high in protein.** A higher intake of dietary protein can improve body composition by increasing the amount of lean muscle tissue in our body, which elevates our resting metabolic rate and increases energy expenditure. It also helps us burn more energy from processing and digesting food, making it easier to maintain a healthy body weight. Dietary protein also aids in appetite control and the amount of food we eat, as it increases the feeling of fullness after eating, again making it easier to maintain a healthier, lower body weight. Protein in our meals also further helps limit the rise in our blood-glucose levels from the carbohydrate sources in the meal.

The CSIRO Low-Carb Diet differs from many other low-carb diets because it is nutritionally complete, providing a healthy balance of carbs, fats, protein and fibre, while minimising the consumption of saturated (unhealthy) fat. The CSIRO Low-Carb Diet includes foods from all the major food groups, with a focus on core, nutrient-dense whole foods, ensuring the diet contains all the essential vitamins, minerals, trace elements and fibre needed for good health.

## Q. HOW DO WE KNOW THE DIET ACTUALLY WORKS? HOW WAS IT TESTED?

*A.* The CSIRO Low-Carb Diet was designed using the latest scientific principles and knowledge of nutrition and dietary factors that promote weight loss, health and wellbeing. The diet was tested in a rigorous two-year clinical trial in 115 adults who were overweight or obese, and had type 2 diabetes. The study found that the CSIRO Low-Carb Diet provided superior benefits to a traditional high-carb, low-fat diet when followed as part of a comprehensive lifestyle plan. The study participants were divided into two dietary groups.

**Group 1** followed an energy-reduced diet that was low in good-quality, unrefined carbohydrate, high in protein and unsaturated fat, and low in saturated fat – in other words, the CSIRO Low-Carb Diet. Of the total daily energy allowance, 14% of kilojoules came from carbohydrate, 28% from protein, and the remaining 58% from fat (with less than 10% from saturated fat).

**Group 2** followed a diet that provided the same amount of energy, but was high in good-quality unrefined carbohydrate (53%), relatively low in protein (17%) and low in fat (30%, with less than 10% saturated fat). This high-carb, low-fat approach has traditionally been recommended by leading health authorities, and is similar to what Australians are typically eating.

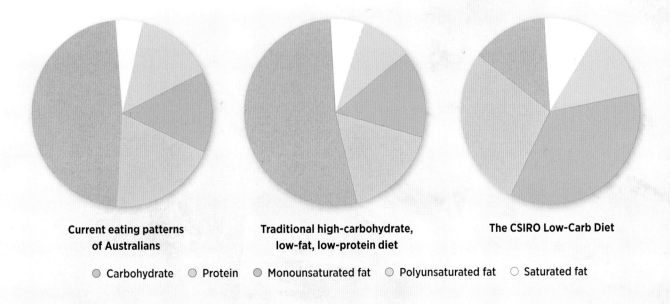

**Current eating patterns of Australians**

**Traditional high-carbohydrate, low-fat, low-protein diet**

**The CSIRO Low-Carb Diet**

○ Carbohydrate      ○ Protein      ○ Monounsaturated fat      ○ Polyunsaturated fat      ○ Saturated fat

Both study groups also participated in the same structured physical activity program, undertaking 60 minutes of combined aerobic and resistance exercise three times every week.

**How the health outcomes were measured:** Before and after the trial, each participant underwent a comprehensive health assessment. Their body weight and composition were recorded (to monitor changes in fat and lean body tissue), along with their blood pressure, blood glucose control, blood lipid profile, kidney function and risk markers for heart disease, to evaluate how each diet affected their health. Changes in their medication requirements were recorded, and mental health and performance were also assessed.

**After 1 year:** It was found that both groups enjoyed substantial and similar reductions in body weight, fat mass, blood pressure, glycated haemoglobin (HbA1c), fasting glucose (clinical measures of blood glucose control) and LDL cholesterol (bad cholesterol), as well as improved mood and quality of life. The level of changes represent clinically relevant improvements in health and wellbeing that significantly reduces the risk of poor health outcomes.

**Benefits enjoyed by both groups** →

| Health measure | Average change in Low-Carb Diet group | Average change in high-carbohydrate group |
|---|---|---|
| Body weight | –9.1% (10 kg) | –9.1% (10 kg) |
| Fat mass | –8.3 kg | –8.3 kg |
| Blood pressure | –6/6 mmHg | –6/6 mmHg |
| HbA1c | –1% (-12.6 mmol/mol) | –1% (-12.6 mmol/mol) |
| Fasting glucose | –1.4 mmol/L | –1.4 mmol/L |
| LDL cholesterol | –0.1 mmol/L | –0.2 mmol/L |
| Mood and quality of life | about 30% improvement | about 30% improvement |

Interestingly, there were **several striking differences** between the two groups for several important health outcomes.

**The low-carb diet group experienced much greater reductions in their need for diabetes medication**, a reduction that was **twice as large** as it was in the high-carb diet group.

**The low-carb diet group also had a greater reduction in blood glucose variation** throughout the day, a reduction that was **three times greater** than in the high-carb group. These greater improvements meant that people in the low-carb group experienced a more stable blood-glucose profile throughout the day (in other words, the degree of excessively high and low blood-glucose levels was reduced). This means better blood-glucose control and lower risk of hypoglycaemia, reduced medication costs and fewer medication side effects. The reduced levels of blood-glucose variation means a lower risk of health complications associated with diabetes.

**The low-carb diet group also had much greater reductions in blood triglyceride levels and increases in HDL-cholesterol (good cholesterol) levels.** This means greater improvement in heart health and lower risk of heart disease.

| Health measure | Average change in the Low-Carb Diet group | Average change in high-carbohydrate group |
|---|---|---|
| Medication requirements* | –40% | –20% |
| Glycaemic variability | –30% | –10% |
| Blood triglycerides | –0.4 mmol/L | –0.01 mmol/L |
| HDL cholesterol | +0.1 mmol/L | +0.06 mmol/L |

**Significant additional benefits of the Low-Carb Diet**

*Medications for controlling blood glucose levels

**After 2 years:** The benefits and differences in health outcomes between the two groups were maintained. This demonstrated that both diets were sustainable and can be followed over the long term to achieve significant health benefits, and also that the superior advantages of the low-carb diet can be maintained.

The study also showed that both the low-carb and high-carb diet had similar effects on cognitive (brain) function, and did not affect clinical markers of renal (kidney) function.

**Overall, these results confirm that the CSIRO Low-Carb Diet is not only an effective weight loss and management approach, but also offers superior benefits for improving blood glucose control and reducing heart disease risk factors, without concerns of negative impact on brain or kidney function.**

## Q. WHO DOES THE LOW-CARB DIET BENEFIT?

A. The CSIRO Low-Carb Diet can be used by a wide cross-section of the community, because it is a dietary pattern that focuses on core nutrient-dense foods and delivers all the essential nutrients – including vitamins, minerals, trace elements and plenty of fibre – required for optimal health.

Many people can benefit from the CSIRO Low-Carb Diet, including those who are overweight or obese and want to lose weight, as well as those simply wanting to improve their diet quality and overall general health.

However, because of the superior benefits for improving blood-glucose control and reducing heart disease risk factors, people with insulin resistance, metabolic syndrome, pre-diabetes and type 2 diabetes will gain extra long-term benefits from adopting the CSIRO Low-Carb Diet and lifestyle plan. And this represents a large and growing portion of society today.

### SHOULD ANYONE AVOID THE CSIRO LOW-CARB DIET?

Until further evidence becomes available, we recommend that people with type 1 diabetes should first consult their healthcare team before trying this dietary approach.

Understandably, there has been great interest in the potential role of a low-carb diet for managing type 1 diabetes, given its demonstrated clinical effectiveness for improving blood glucose control in people with type 2 diabetes, and reducing their need for blood-sugar controlling medication, including insulin.

Anecdotally, some people with type 1 diabetes have reported benefits from eating a diet with reduced carbohydrate. However, to date there is not enough high-quality evidence to inform the role of a low-carb diet in those with type 1 diabetes. More research into the long-term safety and effectiveness of low-carb diets for people with type 1 diabetes is needed.

Low-carb diets are also not recommended at this time for children (anyone under the age of 18) or pregnant women, or people with specialised nutritional requirements.

## Q. WHAT IS THE DIFFERENCE BETWEEN THE CSIRO LOW-CARB DIET AND OTHER CSIRO DIET PLANS?

A. Recognising that 'one size does not fit all', and that there is no single 'magic' diet that will suit every individual's specific needs, the CSIRO has developed a range of scientifically validated dietary programs to suit different eating preferences and health requirements.

Similar to the CSIRO Low-Carb Diet, many of the other CSIRO diet plans, such as the Total Wellbeing Diet and the Healthy Heart Program, are all energy-controlled, high-protein diets and effective weight-management plans.

The key difference is that the CSIRO Low-Carb Diet is substantially lower in carbohydrate, and higher in healthy fats (both monounsaturated and polyunsaturated fat), in order to lower the glycaemic load in the diet and blunt the blood glucose response after eating, while also favourably improving your blood cholesterol profile. In fact, a recent study comparing the effects of diets with different levels of carbohydrate showed that greater increases in blood HDL-cholesterol (good cholesterol) levels and decreases in triglyceride levels occurred with greater carbohydrate restriction.

These improvements are particularly important for reducing the risk of type 2 diabetes, as well as the health complications associated with diabetes and heart disease.

## Q. WHAT DO THE LATEST SCIENTIFIC STUDIES SAY ABOUT LOW-CARB DIETS?

A. Since the release of our CSIRO Low-Carb Diet trial results, several systemic reviews and meta-analyses (combined analytical summaries of several clinical trials examining the same topic) have been published by leading research groups around the world.

The findings from these more recent reviews consistently support our own trial results, demonstrating that low-carb diets are an effective weight-loss strategy, and that in individuals with obesity and type 2 diabetes, they are more effective than a traditional high-carb, low-fat diet in improving glycaemic control and improving blood cholesterol levels, by reducing triglycerides and increasing levels of HDL cholesterol (good cholesterol).

## DIETARY GUIDELINES ARE CHANGING

The strong and growing body of scientific research demonstrating the advantages of a low-carb diet in lowering blood-glucose levels and improving metabolic health has created much international debate among leading health professionals, governing health authorities and the public about the most appropriate dietary approaches for managing pre-diabetes and type 2 diabetes.

This research continues to challenge the traditional recommendation of a high-unrefined-carb, low-fat diet as the only dietary approach, and is leading a global paradigm shift in clinical guidelines for managing type 2 diabetes that has seen a growing acceptance of low-carb diets as an effective dietary plan and treatment option. In fact, the guidelines and position statements of several leading health authorities – including the American Diabetes Association, Diabetes UK, Diabetes Australia, Dietitians Association of Australia and the British Dietetic Association – have been recently amended and updated to endorse the role of low-carb diets as part of an individualised approach to the management of type 2 diabetes.

## Q. DO HIGH-PROTEIN DIETS AFFECT KIDNEY FUNCTION?

*A.* A high-protein diet is believed to place excessive strain on the kidneys and lead to poor kidney function. However, this is only the case for extremely high-protein intakes.

Although the proportion of energy from protein in the CSIRO Low-Carb Diet is higher than in a traditional high-carb diet, the total amount of dietary protein is similar to that in the typical Australian diet – about 100 grams per day.

Our research showed that in people who are overweight or obese with type 2 diabetes who have an increased risk of kidney disease, the CSIRO Low-Carb Diet has similar effects on kidney function as a traditional high-carb, low-protein, low-fat diet.

This result was also confirmed by a 2018 systematic review (a combined analysis of several research studies). Across 12 different studies of almost 1000 patients with type 2 diabetes – including some patients with pre-existing early-stage kidney disease – this analysis showed no differences in the effects on several different measures of kidney function between a low-carb diet and a control diet with a higher proportion of carbohydrate.

Based on these results, we can confidently say the CSIRO Low-Carb Diet will maintain kidney function in people, including those with type 2 diabetes who do not have pre-existing kidney disease.

However, it is still important to start the CSIRO Low-Carb Diet and lifestyle plan in close consultation with your healthcare team, so they can monitor your kidney health. This monitoring is particularly important if you already have type 2 diabetes and/or known kidney impairment, or poor kidney function.

## Q. SHOULD I SEE MY DOCTOR BEFORE STARTING ON THE CSIRO LOW-CARB DIET?

*A.* Before starting any new lifestyle plan that will alter your diet and change your exercise routine, it is recommended that you seek medical advice and have a medical check-up, particularly if you have a current medical condition, or are taking medications for high blood pressure, high cholesterol or diabetes. This is because as the CSIRO Low-Carb Diet can be so effective in improving these health targets, chances are that your medication levels may need to be reduced.

Also, we all have different medical and dietary requirements, so undertaking this diet and lifestyle plan in close consultation with your healthcare team means the plan can be tailored to meet your individual needs. Your healthcare team can also monitor your progress and help maximise the benefits that can be achieved.

In addition to your GP, your healthcare team should include a dietitian or qualified nutritional professional, an exercise physiologist, a psychologist, and a podiatrist if you have been experiencing foot problems. Involving a range of healthcare professionals to support you in your journey can be invaluable, as they can each assist in different ways to individualise aspects of your diet and lifestyle plan, and keep you motivated and on track.

## Q. WHY IS EXERCISE INCLUDED IN THE PLAN?

*A.* The greatest benefits from the CSIRO Low-Carb Diet can be achieved by also participating in regular exercise and enjoying a physically active lifestyle.

This is because evidence consistently shows that participation in regular physical activity is associated with numerous health benefits, regardless of whether you lose weight or not.

**These important health benefits include:**
* better blood glucose control
* a reduced risk of heart disease and premature death
* lower blood pressure and blood fat levels
* a reduced rate of depression, osteoporosis and some forms of cancer.

Research also shows that the level of exercise and physical activity you engage in each week is one of the strongest predictors for successfully maintaining a lower body weight over the long term.

In fact, in the CSIRO's two-year clinical Low-Carb Diet trial, the substantial health improvements were achieved not simply through the participants' diet alone, but because they also engaged in a structured, regular physical activity program, undertaking 60 minutes of combined aerobic and resistance exercise three times per week.

A 2018 study also showed that in people with type 2 diabetes, a low-carb diet had a better glucose-lowering effect than a traditional high-carb (low-GI), low-fat diet, and that these benefits were further magnified when participants also engaged in regular physical activity.

The exercise approach presented in the CSIRO Low-Carb books is a home-based, structured, easy-to-follow plan that incorporates aerobic exercise, resistance (strength) training and flexibility exercises to deliver comprehensive health and wellbeing benefits. These exercise plans are outlined in *The CSIRO Low-Carb Diet* and *CSIRO Low-Carb Every Day* books.

## *Q.* HOW DO I TRACK MY PROGRESS ON THE PLAN?

*A.* Research has shown that monitoring your food intake and exercise levels while regularly tracking your progress and the improvements in your health is a great way to stay motivated and increase your chance of success.

Evidence shows that simply weighing yourself daily can maintain your motivation to stick to a healthy lifestyle, resulting in greater long-term weight-loss success.

It's a great idea to create a food and exercise plan to set your goals, then use this plan and a checklist to check your progress and monitor how closely you are following the plan, so you can make adjustments to help keep you on track.

We have provided online diet and exercise diary templates for you; download these at csiro.au/en/Research/Health/CSIRO-diets/CSIRO-Low-Carb-Diet-Book.

# MAKING IT WORK
## *in your kitchen*

### Q. WHAT WILL I BE EATING ON THE CSIRO LOW-CARB DIET?

**A.** The CSIRO Low-Carb Diet is an energy-controlled, nutritionally complete meal plan that focuses on nutrient-dense whole, core foods, with the majority of kilojoules coming from healthy unsaturated fat and lean protein foods.

Carbohydrate foods are also included, with a focus on high-fibre, low-GI options that are high in resistant starch to promote good bowel health. This includes 50 grams per day of high-fibre, low-GI carbs, with the option, for those needing slightly more carbohydrate over the longer term, of an additional 20 grams of carbohydrate (2 serves) each day, as listed in the table opposite.

Our experience tells us it is better to start with the baseline approach of 50 grams of carbohydrate per day and to then, after a few weeks on the plan, include the extra 20 grams of carbohydrate per day. Or you can simply add the extra 20 grams of good carbs a day as you start to achieve your health and weight loss goal (i.e. if you wish to slow the rate of weight loss), or if you start adding more exercise into your daily routine.

Remember, research shows that this dietary approach can help to control your blood-glucose levels, improve your blood-cholesterol levels and profile, and make weight loss easier – especially if you have pre-diabetes or type 2 diabetes.

### Q. HOW DO I KNOW HOW MUCH OF EACH FOOD GROUP TO EAT?

**A.** We understand that many people find counting calories/kilojoules and grams a bit off-putting, so to make the diet really simple to follow we have sorted foods into different groups based on the nutrients they provide, and assigned the groups a number of 'food units' based on their kilojoule value.

The food groups table on page 26 shows the number of units of each food group you should eat each day, based on the energy level you have selected. Instructions on how to determine your daily energy requirements so that you can select the correct energy level are provided on pages 240–1. Generally, levels 1 and 2 are suitable for women, while levels 3 and 4 are suitable for men.

By eating the correct number of food units each day for your chosen energy level, you are following the CSIRO Low-Carb Diet. It's that simple.

| CARBOHYDRATE EXTRAS | 1 serving = 1 carb extra (10 g carb or less) |
|---|---|
| **FRESH FRUIT – choose most (can be included daily)** | |
| Apples | 50 g |
| Apricots | 2 medium |
| Bananas | 40 g |
| Blueberries, frozen or fresh | 60 g |
| Cherries | 60 g |
| Feijoa | 3 |
| Figs | 2 |
| Kiwifruit | 2 small |
| Lemon or lime juice, freshly squeezed | 300 ml (can add to sparkling water) |
| Nectarine | 1 small |
| Oranges | 100 g |
| Passionfruit | 7 (100 g) |
| Passionfruit pulp (no syrup) | 50 g |
| Peach | 1 small |
| Pears | 50 g |
| Persimmon | 1 small |
| Raspberries, frozen or fresh | 100 g |
| Rhubarb (stewed, no added sugar) | 400 g |
| Strawberries | 200 g |
| **DRIED FRUIT – choose least (once or twice a week)** | |
| Apricots | 20 g |
| Dates | 2 |
| Figs | 1 (20 g) |
| Mixed dried fruit | 10 g |
| Sultanas | 10 g |

There are four energy levels to choose from, offering 6000–9000 kJ per day, that cater for most individual needs. Generally, levels 1 and 2 are suitable for women, while levels 3 and 4 are suitable for men.

| Food groups for the diet | Level 1 (6000 kJ/day) | Level 2 (7000 kJ/day) | Level 3 (8000 kJ/day) | Level 4 (9000 kJ/day) | Key nutrients provided |
|---|---|---|---|---|---|
| Breads, cereals, legumes, starchy vegetables | 1.5 units | 1.5 units | 1.5 units | 1.5 units | Slow-release, low-GI carbohydrates, folate, fibre and B-group vitamins. |
| Lean meat, fish, poultry, eggs, tofu | 1 unit at lunch, 1.5 units at dinner | 1 unit at lunch, 2 units at dinner | 1 unit at lunch, 2.5 units at dinner | 1.5 units at lunch, 2.5 units at dinner | Protein, zinc and vitamin B12. Red meats are highest in iron, fish in omega-3 fatty acids and pork in thiamin. |
| Dairy | 3 units | 3 units | 3.5 units | 4 units | Protein, calcium, vitamin B12 and zinc. Dairy (except most cheeses) also contains carbohydrates. |
| Low–moderate carb vegetables | At least 5 units | At least 5 units | At least 5 units | At least 5 units | Minimal carbohydrates, and plenty of fibre, folate, vitamins A, B6 and C, magnesium, beta-carotene and antioxidants. |
| Healthy fats | 10 units | 11 units | 14 units | 15 units | Vitamins A, E and K, antioxidants and omega-3 and omega-6 fats. |
| **Indulgences** | **2 units per week** | **2 units per week** | **2 units per week** | **2 units per week** | **Limited beneficial nutrients. Most contain added sugars, alcohol and/or saturated fats.** |
| **Carbohydrate extras (Weeks 7+)** | **2 extras per day** | **2 extras per day** | **2 extras per day** | **2 extras per day** | **Carbohydrates. They also contribute vitamins and minerals as they come from your core food units.** |

## To choose which level is right for you...

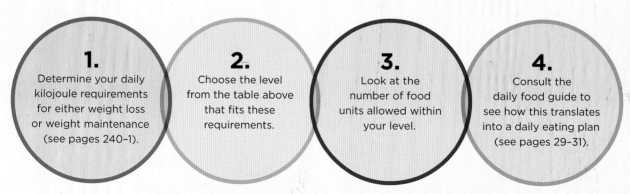

**1.**
Determine your daily kilojoule requirements for either weight loss or weight maintenance (see pages 240–1).

**2.**
Choose the level from the table above that fits these requirements.

**3.**
Look at the number of food units allowed within your level.

**4.**
Consult the daily food guide to see how this translates into a daily eating plan (see pages 29–31).

## Q. CAN YOU TELL ME A BIT MORE ABOUT THE FOOD UNITS?

*A.* To understand what a food unit represents in 'real food' for each category, have a look at the Daily Food Guide on pages 29–31. This guide provides a core list of foods, and explains what quantity of that food represents 1 unit for each food group.

For example, for level 1 – which provides 6000 kJ per day – you'll see that you need to consume 1.5 units from the 'Breads, cereals, legumes, starchy vegetables' group each day. Using the information listed underneath that food group, this means you could, for example, select 30 grams of a suitable cereal (1 unit) and 50 grams of sweet potato (0.5 unit) on a given day. Alternatively, you could obtain your 1.5 units by combining the foods in that category however you like. For example, a combination such as 4 rye Cruskits (1 unit) and 80 grams of cooked, drained lentils (0.5 unit) could be consumed from this food group each day.

This is the great advantage of the CSIRO Low-Carb Diet eating plan: it offers a wide range of choice and flexibility, enabling you to create daily menu plans that suit your food and taste preferences.

By simply making sure that you eat the correct number of food units each day for the energy level selected, and using foods of the type and amount specified in the daily food guide, you can easily 'mix and match' your ingredients and daily menus, knowing you'll still be gaining the full benefit of the CSIRO Low-Carb Diet.

## Q. HOW DO THE RECIPES IN THIS BOOK FIT IN?

*A.* The delicious recipes in this book all align with the key principles of the CSIRO Low-Carb Diet, and use the same food unit system as we've used in our two previous Low-Carb Diet books. Each recipe indicates how many food units it contains, making it simple to incorporate the recipes into your own daily or weekly menu plan.

Importantly, the recipes in this book are quick and easy, making it even simpler to adopt this style of eating into your everyday life.

# Great news FOR VEGGIE LOVERS

Since our last book, we have made a small change to how we categorise some of our high-starch (carbohydrate-rich) veggies.

Green peas, broad beans and pumpkin were previously listed in the 'Low-GI, high-starch vegetable' section in the 'Breads, cereals, legumes, starchy vegetables' food group. Previously, you were allowed a maximum of 1 unit of these veggies a day. We are pleased to let you know that we have moved green peas, broad beans and pumpkin into the moderate carbohydrate vegetables section in the 'Low-moderate carbohydrate vegetables' group – meaning you can increase the number of units of these foods in your daily meal plan. You can now enjoy a new maximum of up to 2 units of these veggies a day, which equates to 1 cup (150 g) of cooked pumpkin, peas or broad beans.

Why, you ask? Green peas, broad beans and pumpkin add valuable fibre to our diet, while broad beans and peas also have the added bonus of containing resistant starch – not to mention that many of our readers have asked to include more of them in the eating plan.

So with this change, please enjoy!

# YOUR DAILY FOOD GUIDE FOR LEVEL 1 (6000 kJ)

The following pages give examples of the types and quantities of foods that can make up your daily intake of units on the diet.

## BREADS, CEREALS, LEGUMES, STARCHY VEGETABLES

**1.5 units per day**

**Choose from:**

1 UNIT HIGH-SOLUBLE-FIBRE, LOW-GI CEREALS

30 g suitable breakfast cereals, such as All-Bran, All-Bran Fibre Toppers, All-Bran Wheat Flakes, Freedom Barley+ Muesli Cranberry, Almond and Cinnamon, Freedom Barley+ Apple and Sultana, Hi-Bran Weet-Bix, untoasted natural muesli, raw natural rolled oats

1 UNIT BREADS

35 g multigrain bread
1 slice (45–50 g) Herman Brot bread
1 thin slice fruit bread
½ wholemeal pita bread (e.g. Mountain Bread wrap)
½ small wholemeal scone (25 g)
3 Ryvitas or 4 rye Cruskits
4 x 9 Grains Vita-Weats

1 UNIT LEGUMES

160 g cooked, drained lentils
80 g cooked, drained chickpeas or red kidney beans
100 g cooked, drained cannellini beans or four-bean mix

1 UNIT LOW-GI, HIGH-STARCH VEGETABLES

100 g sweet potato
70 g corn

1 UNIT GRAINS

15 g wholemeal plain or self-raising flour, cornflour, rice flour, arrowroot or green banana flour
½ cup cooked soba noodles
½ cup cooked low-GI or wholemeal pasta
½ cup cooked quinoa or couscous
⅓ cup cooked low-GI rice

## DAIRY

**3 units per day**

**Choose from:**

1 UNIT DAIRY

150 ml milk or 200 ml skim milk or low-fat calcium-enriched soy or almond milk
80 g natural Greek-style yoghurt or 100 g low-fat natural Greek-style yoghurt or low-fat, lactose-free soy yoghurt
20 g cheddar, parmesan, Swiss or feta cheese
55 g ricotta or cottage cheese
25 g mozzarella or bocconcini cheese, or low-fat cream cheese

# YOUR DAILY FOOD GUIDE FOR LEVEL 1 (6000 kJ)

## LEAN MEAT, FISH, POULTRY, EGGS, TOFU

**2.5 units per day**

**For lunch, choose from:**

1 UNIT LEAN MEAT, FISH, POULTRY, EGGS, TOFU
100 g (cooked weight) lean meat or fish: chicken, turkey, pork, beef, lamb or tinned or fresh fish or seafood
2 eggs (50 g/½ unit each)
100 g tofu (hard or silken)
*We recommend fish for lunch at least twice a week.*

> If you wish to have an egg for breakfast, just have 50 g less meat at lunchtime to account for this.

**For dinner, choose from:**

1.5 UNITS LEAN MEAT, FISH, POULTRY, EGGS, TOFU
150 g (raw weight) lean meat or fish: chicken, turkey, pork, beef, lamb, fish or seafood
3 eggs (50 g/½ unit each)
150 g tofu
*We recommend fish for dinner at least twice a week and red meat no more than three times a week.*

> You may not wish to eat red meat, fish or chicken – or not every day. Legumes are an excellent source of protein for vegetarians or vegans, although they are higher in carbohydrates than their animal-based counterparts, so keep this in mind when planning your daily intake.
> 1 unit of legumes is as follows:
>
> - 160 g cooked, drained lentils (provides 15 g carbs and 11 g protein)
> - 80 g cooked, drained chickpeas or red kidney beans (provides 12 g carbs and 6 g protein)
> - 100 g cooked, drained cannellini beans or four-bean mix (provides 13 g carbs and 6 g protein).

## LOW–MODERATE CARBOHYDRATE VEGETABLES

**At least 5 units per day**

**Choose from:**

1 UNIT LOW-CARBOHYDRATE VEGETABLES
(AT LEAST 3 UNITS OF THESE PER DAY)
½ cup (75 g) cooked vegetables
1 cup (150 g) salad vegetables

*Low-carbohydrate vegetables:* artichoke, asparagus, bean sprouts, broccoli, broccolini, cucumber, garlic, herbs, kale, lettuce, mushrooms, rocket, spices, spinach, tomato and zucchini.

1 UNIT MODERATE-CARBOHYDRATE VEGETABLES
(UP TO 2 UNITS PER DAY)
½ cup (75 g) cooked vegetables
1 cup (150 g) salad vegetables

*Moderate-carbohydrate vegetables:* bamboo shoots, broad beans, brussels sprouts, cabbage, capsicum (all colours), carrot, cauliflower, celery, eggplant, fennel, green beans, green peas, leek, onion, parsnip, pumpkin, radish, spring onion, snowpeas, swede and turnip.

> Strawberries are a very low-carb fruit and can be substituted for a moderate-carb vegetable if you wish (100 g = 1 unit).

> **Note:** Green peas, broad beans and pumpkin are now in this 'Low–moderate carbohydrate vegetables' category. You can enjoy a maximum of up to 2 units of these veggies a day, which equates to 1 cup (150 g) of cooked peas, broad beans or pumpkin. See page 28 for more details.

# HEALTHY FATS

**10 units a day**

## Choose from:

1 UNIT HEALTHY FATS

5 g (1 teaspoon) olive, grapeseed or sunflower oil

5 g (1 teaspoon) tahini (sesame butter)

20 g avocado

20 g (1 tablespoon) hummus

5 g (1 teaspoon) olive oil, canola or Nuttelex margarine

10 g nuts (almonds, cashews, pecans or walnuts)

10 g almond meal

10 g (1 teaspoon) whole-egg mayonnaise

> Nuts are a primary source of healthy fats in the Low-Carb Diet. We encourage you to eat at least 60 g (6 units) of nuts each day.

# Indulgence foods

**2 units per week**

## Choose from:

1 UNIT INDULGENCE FOOD

Any food or drink providing approximately 450 kJ – e.g. 150 ml wine, 20 g chocolate, 40 g store-bought low-fat dips, 10 Arnotts Shapes, 1 x 20 g packet of chips, 10 Pringles, ½ slice of pizza or 35 g hot chips.

## Q. HOW DO I DETERMINE MY DAILY ENERGY REQUIREMENTS?

*A.* Now that you understand the food units, how much of each food group you need each day, and how flexible and adaptable this system is, the next step is to calculate the right energy level for you, by determining your energy (kilojoule) requirements. To do this, simply refer to pages 240–1.

## Q. HOW CAN I INTEGRATE THIS DIET INTO MY BUSY LIFE?

*A.* One of the best ways to set yourself up for success is to plan ahead. This way you'll have everything ready and in place to keep you on track, making the CSIRO Low-Carb Diet an easy part of your everyday life.

**Prepare your kitchen:** look through the recipes and ensure you have all the basic equipment, such as utensils and cookware. Having everything you need at your fingertips means you'll be able to prepare all the recipes with ease.

**Prepare your pantry:** ensure you have all the food you need in the pantry, freezer and fridge to make your delicious low-carb recipes. This includes all your favourite herbs and spices, to bring out all those fabulous food flavours.

**Prepare daily snacks and meals in advance:** keep the kitchen stocked with a variety of healthy snack options as part of the diet plan. Stock the freezer with a few ready-made meals from the plan as an emergency option for when things don't go to plan and you don't have time to cook.

> The following pages contain lots of great tips for building healthy meals from 'the ground up' on those days when you don't want to follow a recipe. There are 16 meal-builder ideas, but if you mix and match, the possibilities are endless! You'll also find quick and easy ideas for low-carb-friendly pizzas, soups and drinks.

# HOW DO I GET STARTED ON THE CSIRO LOW-CARB DIET PLAN?

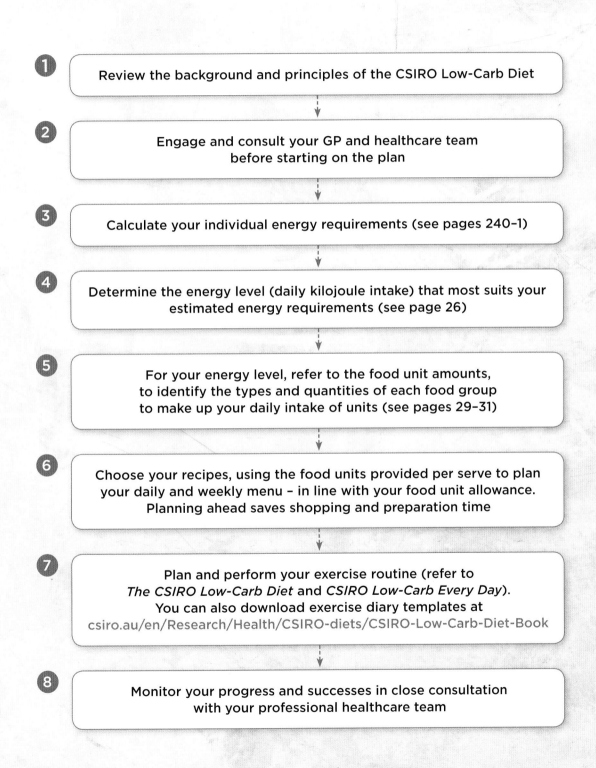

**1** Review the background and principles of the CSIRO Low-Carb Diet

**2** Engage and consult your GP and healthcare team before starting on the plan

**3** Calculate your individual energy requirements (see pages 240–1)

**4** Determine the energy level (daily kilojoule intake) that most suits your estimated energy requirements (see page 26)

**5** For your energy level, refer to the food unit amounts, to identify the types and quantities of each food group to make up your daily intake of units (see pages 29–31)

**6** Choose your recipes, using the food units provided per serve to plan your daily and weekly menu – in line with your food unit allowance. Planning ahead saves shopping and preparation time

**7** Plan and perform your exercise routine (refer to *The CSIRO Low-Carb Diet* and *CSIRO Low-Carb Every Day*). You can also download exercise diary templates at csiro.au/en/Research/Health/CSIRO-diets/CSIRO-Low-Carb-Diet-Book

**8** Monitor your progress and successes in close consultation with your professional healthcare team

# EGG TOAST TOPPERS *meal builders*

On average, each combination provides 15 g of carbohydrate.

**1** 1 egg, scrambled

20 g Swiss cheese slice

20 g avocado

**2** 1 egg, soft boiled

20 g reduced-fat feta

1 teaspoon tahini

**3** 1 egg, poached

20 g parmesan, shaved

1 teaspoon fresh basil pesto

1 TSP

**4** 1 egg, hardboiled

25 g reduced-fat cream cheese

20 g pitted green Sicilian olives, quartered

**5** 1 egg, dry, pan-fried

55 g reduced-fat fresh ricotta

10 g toasted pine nuts

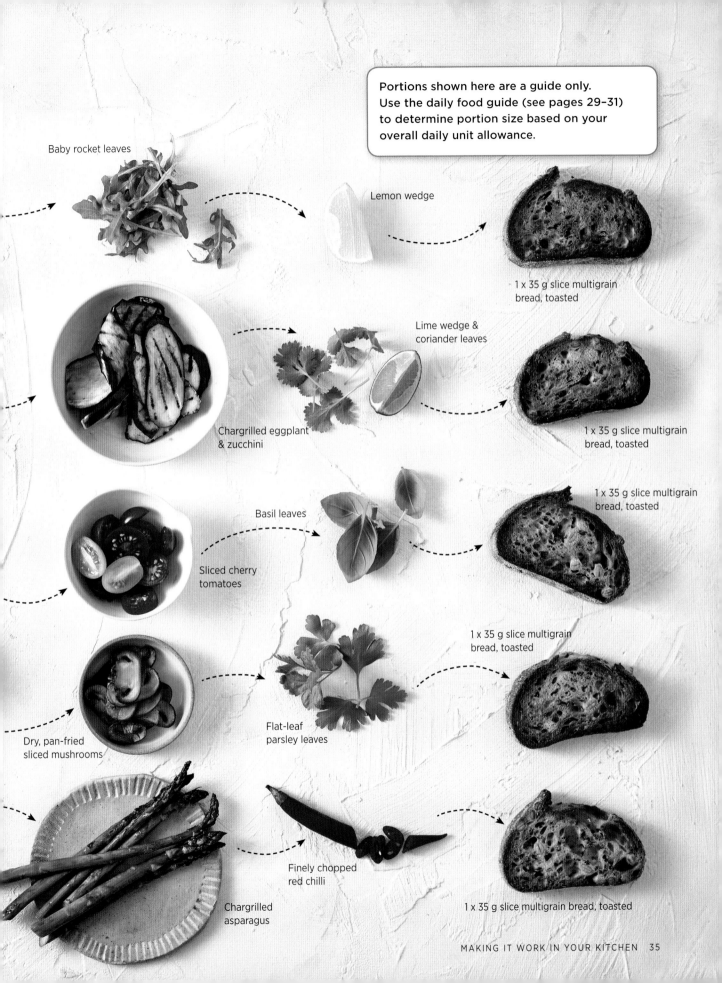

Baby rocket leaves

Lemon wedge

1 x 35 g slice multigrain bread, toasted

Portions shown here are a guide only. Use the daily food guide (see pages 29–31) to determine portion size based on your overall daily unit allowance.

Chargrilled eggplant & zucchini

Lime wedge & coriander leaves

1 x 35 g slice multigrain bread, toasted

Sliced cherry tomatoes

Basil leaves

1 x 35 g slice multigrain bread, toasted

Dry, pan-fried sliced mushrooms

Flat-leaf parsley leaves

1 x 35 g slice multigrain bread, toasted

Chargrilled asparagus

Finely chopped red chilli

1 x 35 g slice multigrain bread, toasted

# FRUIT BREAKFAST *meal builders*

On average, each combination provides 22 g of carbohydrate.

**1** 30 g All-Bran Fibre Toppers → 200 g reduced-fat plain yoghurt → 1 teaspoon cashew butter

**2** 30 g Hi-Bran Weet-Bix → 200 ml plain reduced-fat milk → 10 g pistachios, chopped

**3** 25 g (½) wholemeal scone → 55 g cottage cheese → 10 g slivered almonds, toasted

**4** 30 g untoasted natural muesli → 200 ml plain reduced-fat milk → 10 g pepitas

**5** 1 thin (30 g) slice fruit bread, toasted → 55 g reduced-fat fresh ricotta → 1 teaspoon almond butter

Portions shown here are a guide only.
Use the daily food guide (see pages 29–31)
to determine portion size based on your
overall daily unit allowance.

80 g sliced strawberries

Ground turmeric

80 g mixed
fresh berries

Finely chopped mint

80 g frozen
blackberries

Finely grated
lemon rind

80 g fresh
blueberries

Ground cinnamon

Fresh lemon
thyme leaves

80 g fresh
raspberries

# PITA BREAD PIZZA FOR TWO *meal builders*

On average, each serve (½ pita bread with toppings) provides 19 g of carbohydrate.

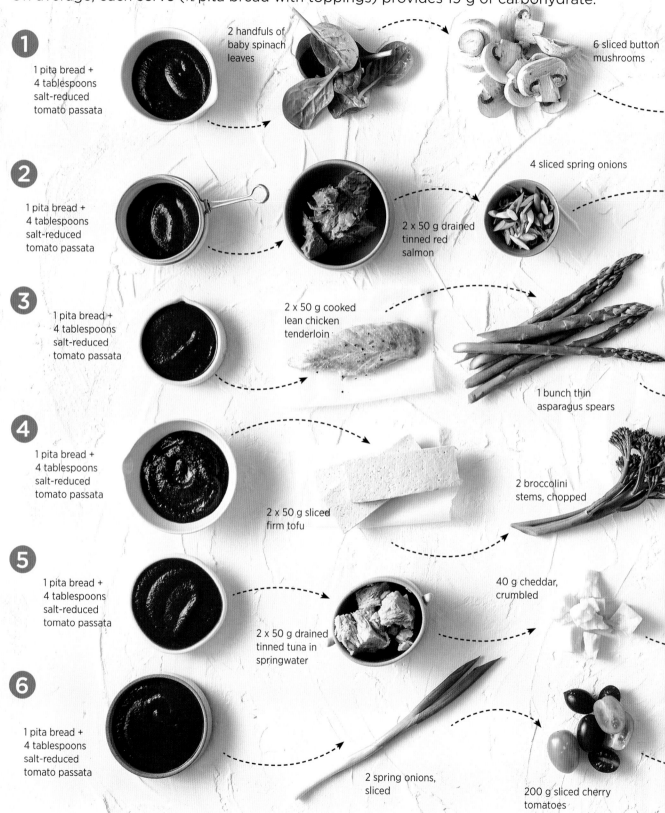

**1** 1 pita bread + 4 tablespoons salt-reduced tomato passata

2 handfuls of baby spinach leaves

6 sliced button mushrooms

**2** 1 pita bread + 4 tablespoons salt-reduced tomato passata

2 x 50 g drained tinned red salmon

4 sliced spring onions

**3** 1 pita bread + 4 tablespoons salt-reduced tomato passata

2 x 50 g cooked lean chicken tenderloin

1 bunch thin asparagus spears

**4** 1 pita bread + 4 tablespoons salt-reduced tomato passata

2 x 50 g sliced firm tofu

2 broccolini stems, chopped

**5** 1 pita bread + 4 tablespoons salt-reduced tomato passata

2 x 50 g drained tinned tuna in springwater

40 g cheddar, crumbled

**6** 1 pita bread + 4 tablespoons salt-reduced tomato passata

2 spring onions, sliced

200 g sliced cherry tomatoes

Portions shown here are a guide only. Use the daily food guide (see pages 29–31) to determine portion size based on your overall daily unit allowance.

2 x 50 g cooked lean chicken tenderloin

50 g torn bocconcini

40 g pitted, quartered kalamata olives and a handful of small basil leaves

50 g grated mozzarella

2 small handfuls of baby rocket

4 teaspoons fresh basil pesto

110 g reduced-fat fresh ricotta

fresh thyme leaves

4 cloves garlic, sliced

2 tablespoons extra virgin olive oil

20 g toasted slivered almonds

2 Lebanese cucumbers, peeled into long thin lengths

mint leaves

40 g reduced-fat feta, crumbled

lime wedges

2 small handfuls of torn kale leaves

sliced red chilli

flat-leaf parsley leaves

40 g parmesan, grated

80 g sliced avocado

2 hardboiled eggs

baby cos leaves

PITA BREAD PIZZA FOR TWO *meal builders*

## Method for cooking pizzas

1. Preheat the oven to 220°C/200°C fan-forced. Line a large baking tray with baking paper.
2. Place the prepared pita bread pizzas on the prepared tray.
3. Bake for 8–12 minutes or until the base is crisp and the toppings are cooked and golden.

Portions shown here are a guide only.
Use the daily food guide (see pages 29–31)
to determine portion size based on your
overall daily unit allowance.

# SIMPLE SOUPS FOR LUNCH

On average, each serve provides 20 g of carbohydrate.

## LEMONY CHICKEN, BEAN AND BROCCOLI

**Serves 1**

Cook 50 g lean chicken tenderloin in a non-stick frying pan over high heat for 6 minutes until golden and cooked, then chop.

Boil together 1½ cups (375 ml) salt-reduced chicken stock; 300 g chopped broccoli florets and 100 g drained tinned cannellini beans for 5 minutes until broccoli is just cooked.

Stir through chicken; finely grated zest and juice of 1 small lemon and ¼ cup chopped fresh flat-leaf parsley leaves. Serve.

## MEXICAN CHICKEN

**Serves 1**

Cook 50 g lean chicken tenderloin in a non-stick frying pan over high heat for 6 minutes until golden and cooked, then chop.

Boil together 1½ cups (375 ml) salt-reduced chicken stock; ½ cup tomato salsa; 1 teaspoon Mexican chilli powder; 80 g drained tinned red kidney beans and 300 g chopped zucchini for 8 minutes until zucchini is cooked.

Stir through chicken and finely grated zest and juice of 1 lime.

Serve topped with 80 g chopped avocado and small fresh coriander leaves.

## SPICED CHICKEN AND ASPARAGUS

**Serves 1**

Cook 50 g lean chicken tenderloin in a non-stick frying pan over high heat for 6 minutes until golden and cooked, then chop.

Boil together 1½ cups (375 ml) salt-reduced chicken stock; 1 bunch chopped asparagus; 1 spring onion and 1 teaspoon harissa paste for 5 minutes until asparagus is just tender.

Stir in chicken. Top with fresh mint leaves.

Serve with 4 x 9 Grains Vita-Weats spread with 1 tablespoon hummus.

### DHAL SOUP WITH EGG

**Serves 1**

Cook 1 x 55 g egg in boiling water for 8 minutes until hard boiled. Drain and cool under running water before peeling. Cut into wedges, set aside.

Boil together 1½ cups (375 ml) salt-reduced vegetable stock; 30 g dried split red lentils; 2 teaspoons korma curry paste and 150 g chopped zucchini for 12 minutes until lentils are soft.

Stir through 1 cup baby spinach leaves until wilted.

Serve topped with boiled egg and finely chopped fresh chives and finely chopped fresh coriander leaves.

### ITALIAN TUNA AND RISONI

**Serves 1**

Boil together 1½ cups (375 ml) salt-reduced chicken stock; 30 g dried risoni pasta; 150 g shredded green cabbage and 1 chopped tomato for 8 minutes until risoni is cooked.

Serve topped with 50 g drained tinned tuna in springwater and 2 teaspoons fresh basil pesto.

### SALMON CHOWDER

**Serves 1**

Boil together 1½ cups (375 ml) salt-reduced chicken stock; 100 g peeled, finely chopped potato; 150 g chopped cauliflower florets and 150 g chopped zucchini for 10 minutes until tender. Blend until smooth.

Serve topped with 50 g drained tinned red salmon; 10 g toasted pepitas and 1 tablespoon fresh dill leaves.

Portions shown here are a guide only. Use the daily food guide (see pages 29–31) to determine portion size based on your overall daily unit allowance.

# DRINKS

**7 G CARB**

### GREEN SMOOTHIE

**Serves 1 as a between-meal top-up**

Blend together ½ Lebanese cucumber, ½ peeled lime, 1 handful baby spinach leaves, 1 large handful fresh mint leaves, 40 g frozen raspberries and 200 ml chilled water until smooth. Serve with 10 g pepitas.

2 UNITS LOW–MOD-CARB VEG
1 UNIT HEALTHY FAT

**2 G CARB**

### ASIAN CHICKEN BROTH

**Serves 1 as a between-meal top-up**

Place ½ handful baby spinach leaves, 2 teaspoons salt-reduced soy sauce and 1 teaspoon grated fresh ginger in a mug. Pour over 200 ml heated salt-reduced chicken stock and stir well to combine. Serve with ½ teaspoon toasted sesame seeds.

1 UNIT LOW–MOD-CARB VEG
1 UNIT HEALTHY FAT

**20 G CARB**

### CHOC-MOUSSE MORNING SHAKE

**Serves 1 as a breakfast replacement**

Blend together 3 teaspoons diet chocolate topping, 200 ml reduced-fat milk, 40 g avocado flesh and 30 g All-Bran Fibre Toppers until smooth, then serve.

1 UNIT BREADS/CEREALS
1 UNIT DAIRY
2 UNITS HEALTHY FATS

**2 G CARB**

## ICED VANILLA COFFEE

**Serves 1**

Combine 3 teaspoons instant coffee powder, 1 split vanilla pod and 200 ml boiling water in a heatproof jug. Leave to stand for 5 minutes to infuse, stirring occasionally. Fill a glass with ice and pour over the coffee mixture, inserting the vanilla pod. Serve as is or add 1 tablespoon of reduced-fat milk.

**2 G CARB**

## MORNING BOOSTER

**Serves 1**

Place the finely grated zest and juice of 1 small lemon in a mug along with 1 teaspoon grated fresh ginger, ½ teaspoon ground turmeric and 1 chai tea bag. Pour over ⅔ cup (180 ml) boiling water and stir to combine. Leave to steep for 4 minutes before drinking.

**0.5 UNIT LOW–MOD-CARB VEG**

**10 G CARB**

## CARAMEL ALMOND LATTE

**Serves 1**

Place 2 teaspoons diet caramel topping and 2 teaspoons instant coffee powder in a heatproof serving glass. Pour over 200 ml warmed calcium-enriched almond milk. Stir well to combine, then top with 2 teaspoons almond butter and a pinch of mixed spice.

**1 UNIT DAIRY**
**2 UNITS HEALTHY FATS**

Portions shown here are a guide only. Use the daily food guide (see pages 29–31) to determine portion size based on your overall daily unit allowance.

# WEEKLY MEAL *Plan 1*

Based on energy level 1 (6000 kJ per day).

| | MONDAY | TUESDAY | WEDNESDAY | THURSDAY |
|---|---|---|---|---|
| **BREAKFAST** | 30 g grilled haloumi, 75 g grilled mushrooms and 75 g blanched spinach served with 60 g sliced avocado on 1 slice Herman Brot Lower Carb Bread | 100 g reduced-fat natural or Greek-style yoghurt with 20 g mixed nuts and seeds | 30 g untoasted natural muesli topped with 100 g reduced-fat natural or Greek-style yoghurt and 30 g mixed nuts and seeds | 60 g grilled haloumi + 1 cup grilled vegetables blended with 20 g nut or seed butter (e.g. tahini or macadamia paste) |
| **LUNCH** | Chicken and Green Olive Couscous Salad (page 62) | Hearty Fish Soup (page 101) | Four-bean Bolognese (page 72) | Chicken Pita with Zucchini Salad (page 89) |
| **DINNER** | Pepper Steak Mushroom Melt (page 144) | Almond-crusted Chicken and Broccoli Bake (page 186) | Pumpkin and Tofu Tagine (page 196) | Greek Lamb and Eggplant Wraps (page 216) |
| **DAILY CORE SNACKS** | Cheese plate for 1: 20 g cubed cheddar, 40 g mixed nuts, 50 g grilled artichoke hearts and 2 small Lebanese cucumbers, sliced | 2 wholegrain Vita-Weats topped with 2 teaspoons tahini, 20 g avocado and 20 g cheddar | 1 rye Cruskit topped with 20 g cheddar + 40 g mixed nuts | 100 g reduced-fat natural or Greek-style yoghurt topped with 15 g high-fibre cereal, 30 g mixed nuts and seeds and 50 g fresh or frozen berries |
| **DAILY CARB TOTAL** | 51 g | 48 g | 52 g | 45 g |

**DAILY UNIT TARGETS:**
Breads, cereals, legumes, starchy vegetables: **1.5 (nil to be used in the dinner meals)**
Dairy and dairy alternatives: **3**
Lean meat, fish, poultry, eggs, tofu: **2.5 (must have 1.5 for dinner)**
Low–moderate carb vegetables: **5 minimum (3 minimum from low-carb varieties)**
Healthy fats: **10**

|  | FRIDAY | SATURDAY | SUNDAY |
|---|---|---|---|
| **BREAKFAST** | **FRANTIC FRIDAY GRAB AND GO:**<br>1 Ryvita topped with 20 g cheddar and 1 medium sliced tomato + 30 g nuts | **OUT AND ABOUT:**<br>1 small coffee or tea (125 ml milk) + 1 tablespoon nut-based granola or clusters mixed with 40 g nuts and seeds (packed into a small container to take with you) | **SLEEPY SUNDAY:**<br>1 slice Herman Brot Lower Carb Bread spread with 1 tablespoon hummus, topped with 40 g sliced avocado, 1 medium sliced tomato and 20 g cheddar.<br>Grill and serve |
| **LUNCH** | **Speedy Fish Pie** (page 70) | **Chicken Caesar Burger** (page 88) | **Vegetable Frying-pan Pie** (page 84) |
| **DINNER** | **Fennel Pork with Beetroot Ceviche** (page 236) | **Beef and Pumpkin Massaman** (page 169) | **Soy Baked Fish Parcels** (page 232) |
| **DAILY CORE SNACKS** | 50 g pecans and almonds | Cheese plate for 1: 20 g cubed cheddar, 40 g mixed nuts, 50 g grilled artichoke hearts, 2 small Lebanese cucumbers, sliced, and 50 g strawberries | 100 g reduced-fat natural or Greek-style yoghurt + 50 g slivered almonds |
| **DAILY CARB TOTAL** | 50 g | 50 g | 45 g |

# WEEKLY MEAL *Plan 2*

Breakfast and snacks are often similar day in and day out. Therefore, this second meal plan aims to demonstrate how we can make minor changes to these times and still use the recipes to get the best variety. Based on energy level 1 (6000 kJ per day).

| | MONDAY | TUESDAY | WEDNESDAY | THURSDAY |
|---|---|---|---|---|
| **BREAKFAST** | 30 g grilled haloumi, 75 g grilled mushrooms and 75 g blanched spinach served with 60 g sliced avocado on 1 slice Herman Brot Lower Carb Bread | 100 g reduced-fat natural or Greek-style yoghurt with 50 g mixed fresh or frozen berries | 15 g untoasted natural muesli topped with 100 g reduced-fat natural or Greek-style yoghurt and sprinkled with 30 g mixed nuts and seeds | 30 g grilled haloumi + 1 cup grilled vegetables blended with 20 g nut or seed butter (e.g. tahini or macadamia paste) served on 1 slice Herman Brot Lower Carb Bread |
| **LUNCH** | **Antipasto Chicken Pasta** (page 80) | **Egg Salad with Feta Dressing** (page 73) | **Tuna Pesto Pasta Salad** (page 65) | **Curried Chickpea and Chicken Salad** (page 96) |
| **DINNER** | **Sumac beef and zucchini mint salad** (page 239) | **Ricotta-stuffed Chicken with Vegetable Medley** (page 215) | **Barbecued Salsa Verde Lamb** (page 138) | **Greek Lamb and Bean Salad** (page 182) |
| **DAILY CORE SNACKS** | 40 g mixed nuts (e.g. 10 g almonds, 10 g pecans, 10 g walnuts, 10 g pistachios) + 20 g dried wasabi peas | 5 wholegrain rice crackers, 3 chopped baby Lebanese cucumbers, 5 cherry tomatoes, 20 g mixed nuts and 40 g hummus | 40 g mixed nuts and 50 g mixed fresh or frozen berries | 25 g mixed nuts and seeds, 5 wholegrain rice crackers and 50 g mixed fresh or frozen berries OR 1 cup chopped low-moderate carb veggies |
| **DAILY CARB TOTAL** | 49 g | 51 g | 46 g | 45 g |

**DAILY UNIT TARGETS:**
Breads, cereals, legumes, starchy vegetables: **1.5 (nil to be used in the dinner meals)**
Dairy and dairy alternatives: **3**
Lean meat, fish, poultry, eggs, tofu: **2.5 (must have 1.5 for dinner)**
Low-moderate carb vegetables: **5 minimum (3 minimum from low-carb varieties)**
Healthy fats: **10**

| | FRIDAY | SATURDAY | SUNDAY |
|---|---|---|---|
| **BREAKFAST** | **FRANTIC FRIDAY GRAB AND GO:**<br>1 Ryvita topped with 20 g cheddar and 1 medium sliced tomato + 30 g nuts | **OUT AND ABOUT:**<br>1 small coffee or tea (125 ml milk) + 1 tablespoon nut-based granola or clusters mixed with 40 g nuts and seeds (packed into a small container to take with you) | **SLEEPY SUNDAY:**<br>1 slice Herman Brot Lower Carb Bread spread with 1 tablespoon hummus, topped with 40 g sliced avocado, 1 medium sliced tomato and 20 g cheddar. Grill and serve |
| **LUNCH** | Flathead and Warm Vegetable Salsa (page 87) | Chicken Chow Mein (page 75) | Tomato and Chicken Salad with Avo Toasts (page 102) |
| **DINNER** | Chermoula Chicken and Vegetables (page 140) | Barbecued Beef with Chimichurri Pickled Vegetables (page 219) | Beef Steak and Panang Vegetables (page 185), served with a side of green beans and asparagus |
| **DAILY CORE SNACKS** | Cheese plate for 1: 40 g pecans and almonds, 30 g cubed cheddar, 1 cup chopped low–moderate carb veggies and 40 g fresh strawberries | 200 g reduced-fat natural or Greek-style yoghurt topped with 10 g mixed seeds | 100 g reduced-fat natural or Greek-style yoghurt blended with + 100 g mixed fresh or frozen berries, then topped with 10 g mixed seeds or nuts |
| **DAILY CARB TOTAL** | 46 g | 52 g | 47 g |

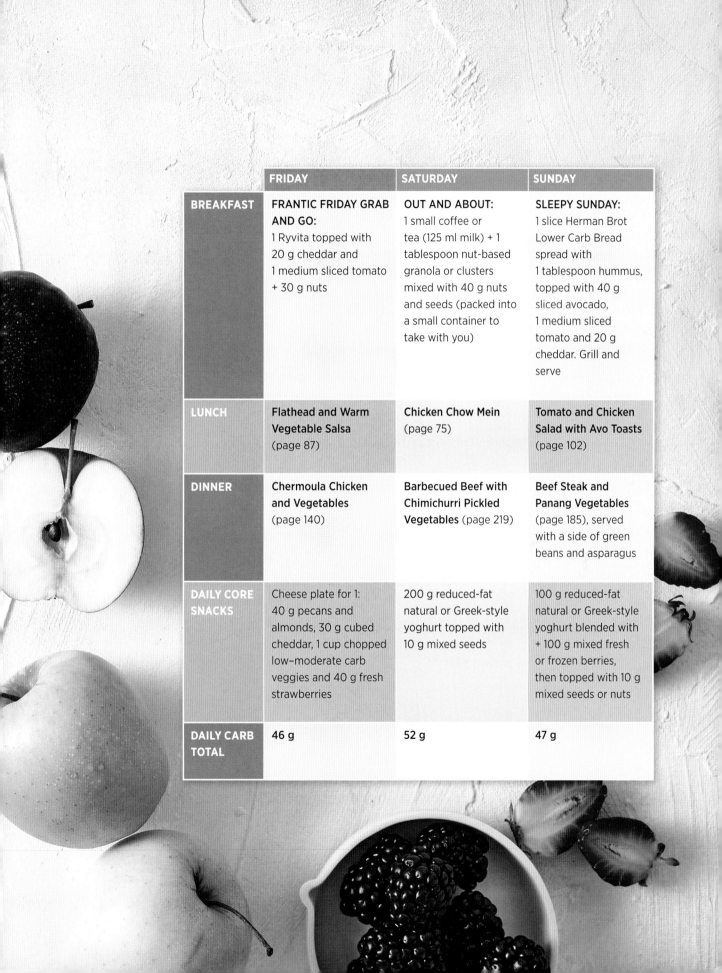

# Meal plan 1 Shopping list

| QUANTITY | ITEM | QUANTITY | ITEM |
|---|---|---|---|
| ........ | lean beef strips | | baby fennel |
| ........ | skinless, boneless snapper fillets | ........ | beetroot |
| ........ | skinless, boneless white fish fillets | ........ | choy sum |
| ........ | thick-cut skinless, boneless barramundi fillets | ........ | red capsicum |
| ........ | lean chicken breast fillet stir-fry strips | ........ | spring onions |
| ........ | lean uncrumbed chicken breast | ........ | broccoli florets |
| ........ | schnitzel steaks | ........ | eggplants |
| ........ | lean pork medallions | ........ | pumpkin |
| ........ | lean lamb backstrap | ........ | mushrooms |
| ........ | firm tofu | ........ | coriander |
| ........ | strawberries | ........ | basil |
| ........ | berries (optional – can use frozen) | ........ | chives |
| ........ | lemons | ........ | low–moderate carb veggies for grilling |
| ........ | tomatoes | ........ | packet traditional vegetables stir-fry mix |
| ........ | avocado | ........ | packet mixed leaf iceberg lettuce blend |
| ........ | artichoke hearts | ........ | packet Greek-style salad kit |
| ........ | Lebanese cucumbers | ........ | packet fresh zucchini spaghetti |
| ........ | English spinach | ........ | pitted green olives |
| ........ | baby spinach | ........ | haloumi |
| ........ | baby rocket leaves | ........ | parmesan |
| ........ | red onions | ........ | cheddar |
| ........ | zucchini | ........ | baby bocconcini |
| ........ | sticks celery | ........ | mozzarella |
| ........ | carrots | ........ | reduced-fat cream cheese |
| ........ | leek | ........ | |

# Meal plan 2 Shopping list

| QUANTITY | ITEM | QUANTITY | ITEM |
|---|---|---|---|
| . . . . . . . . | trimmed beef topside | . . . . . . . . | small baby potatoes |
| . . . . . . . | lean beef minute steaks | . . . . . . . | bok choy |
| . . . . . . . | lean beef fillet steaks | . . . . . . . | eggplants |
| . . . . . . . | lean chicken breast fillets | . . . . . . . | broccoli florets |
| . . . . . . . | lean chicken breast | . . . . . . . | cauliflower florets |
| . . . . . . . | lean chicken tenderloins | . . . . . . . | leek |
| . . . . . . . | lean chicken breast fillet stir-fry strips | . . . . . . . | thin asparagus |
| . . . . . . . | heart-smart lamb | . . . . . . . | broccolini |
| . . . . . . . | extra-trim Frenched lamb cutlets | . . . . . . . | baby green beans |
| . . . . . . . | skinless, boneless flathead fillets | . . . . . . . | flat-leaf parsley |
| . . . . . . . | strawberries | . . . . . . . | coriander |
| . . . . . . . | mixed berries (optional – can use frozen) | . . . . . . . | basil |
| . . . . . . . | lemons | . . . . . . . | mint |
| . . . . . . . | limes | . . . . . . . | low–moderate carb veggies for snacking/grilling |
| . . . . . . . | cherry tomatoes | . . . . . . . | fresh basil pesto |
| . . . . . . . | tomatoes | . . . . . . . | fresh salsa verde |
| . . . . . . . | avocado | . . . . . . . | packet Greek-style salad kit |
| . . . . . . . | baby cucumbers | . . . . . . . | packet chopped mixed kale mix |
| . . . . . . . | baby button mushrooms | . . . . . . . | packet zucchini spaghetti |
| . . . . . . . | baby rocket leaves | . . . . . . . | green olives stuffed with feta |
| . . . . . . . | baby spinach | . . . . . . . | mixed Tuscan antipasto |
| . . . . . . . | mixed salad leaves | . . . . . . . | small low-GI pasta shells |
| . . . . . . . | iceberg lettuce | . . . . . . . | dried wasabi peas |
| . . . . . . . | zucchini | . . . . . . . | haloumi |
| . . . . . . . | spring onions | . . . . . . . | parmesan |
| | | . . . . . . . | cheddar |
| | | . . . . . . . | baby bocconcini |

# Pantry staples

untoasted natural muesli

high-fibre cereal

nut-based granola or clusters

almond meal

almonds (whole and slivered)

pecans

pistachios

walnuts

mixed nuts and seeds

tahini (optional, macadamia paste)

small wholemeal pita breads, torn

multigrain sourdough bread

Herman Brot Lower Carb Bread

mixed seed and grain sandwich thins

Ryvita

Vita-Weats

Cruskits

wholegrain rice crackers

wholemeal spaghetti

Wholemeal couscous

dried brown rice noodles

salt-reduced chicken stock

salt-reduced vegetable stock

salt-reduced tomato paste

tinned chopped tomatoes (regular, rich and thick mixed herbs, rich and thick basil and garlic)

tinned chickpeas

tinned tuna in springwater

tinned four-bean mix

## SAUCES AND CONDIMENTS

sunflower oil

olive oil

extra virgin olive oil

sesame oil

fat-free French dressing

fat-free Caesar dressing

fat-free Greek salad dressing

mild chunky tomato salsa

white wine vinegar

red wine vinegar

salt-reduced soy sauce

hoisin sauce

## HERBS, SPICES AND SEASONING

garlic

ginger

fresh garlic paste

fresh coriander herb paste

fresh parsley herb paste

fresh Italian spice paste

onion, garlic and Italian herb paste

dried chilli flakes

dried Italian herbs

dried mixed herbs

sumac

fennel seeds

cayenne pepper

curry powder

sweet paprika

Mexican chilli powder

Moroccan seasoning

pepper steak seasoning

no-added-salt garlic and herb seasoning

harissa seasoning

panang curry paste

massaman curry paste

## FRIDGE

milk

eggs

hummus

reduced-fat natural or Greek-style yoghurt

reduced-fat fresh ricotta

reduced-fat Greek feta

## FREEZER

frozen peas, corn and carrot

frozen broccoli and cauliflower rice

frozen steam fresh beans, broccoli and sugar snap peas

frozen broad beans, shelled

frozen stir-fry Chinese Vegetables

frozen Thai-style stir-fry vegetables

frozen mixed berries

> Some of our recipes make use of pre-packaged salad mixes and pre-mixed pastes and pestos to save you even more time in the kitchen. These are readily available at major supermarkets and the units have been calculated on these specific products.

PART 2

# QUICK AND EASY
## Recipes

Lean meat, fish, poultry, eggs, tofu: **1**
Breads, cereals, legumes, starchy
    vegetables: **1**
Dairy and dairy alternatives: **1**
Low-moderate carb vegetables: **3**
Healthy fats: **2**

# PESTO CHICKEN AND VEGGIE MELTS

23 G CARB PER SERVE

🍴 **Serves 4**   🕐 **Preparation: 20 minutes**
🍲 **Cooking: 20 minutes**   ⏱ **Difficulty: Low**

400 g lean chicken tenderloins, sliced
    diagonally and seasoned with pepper
2 eggplants, sliced
2 zucchini, thinly sliced diagonally
2 bunches thin asparagus, trimmed
4 x 35 g slices multigrain bread, toasted
4 tomatoes, sliced
100 g mozzarella, grated
2 tablespoons fresh basil pesto

Heat a large chargrill pan over high heat. Add half the chicken and cook, turning occasionally, for 5 minutes or until golden and cooked through. Transfer to a plate and repeat with the remaining chicken.

Chargrill the eggplant, zucchini and asparagus in two batches for 3 minutes each, turning occasionally, until golden and just tender.

Preheat the oven grill to high. Place the toast on a large baking tray. Top with the tomato, chargrilled vegetables and chargrilled chicken and sprinkle with the mozzarella. Grill for 2–3 minutes or until the cheese is melted and golden.

Drizzle with the pesto and serve warm.

**24 G CARB PER SERVE**

**UNITS PER SERVE**

Lean meat, fish, poultry, eggs, tofu: **1**

Breads, cereals, legumes, starchy
  vegetables: **1**

Dairy and dairy alternatives: **0**

Low–moderate carb vegetables: **1**

Healthy fats: **2**

🍴 **Serves 4**   🕐 **Preparation: 10 minutes**
🍲 **Cooking: 20 minutes**   ⏱ **Difficulty: Medium**

4 x 100 g skinless, boneless salmon
  fillets

¼ cup (60 g) fresh Moroccan
  spice paste

80 g Doongara (low GI) clever
  white rice

1 cup (250 ml) salt-reduced
  chicken stock

1 x 450 g packet frozen steamed beans,
  broccoli and sugar snap peas

40 g slivered almonds, toasted

small coriander sprigs and lime wedges,
  to serve

Combine the salmon and spice paste in a bowl until well coated.
Heat a large, deep non-stick frying pan over medium–high heat.
Add the salmon and turn to brown on all sides. Remove to a plate.

Reduce the heat to medium–low. Add the rice and stock to the
pan and simmer, stirring occasionally, for 10 minutes or until the
stock has reduced by two-thirds. Add the vegetables and salmon,
then simmer for 6–8 minutes or until the stock has been completely
absorbed, the rice is tender and the salmon is cooked.

Sprinkle with the slivered almonds and coriander sprigs and serve
straight from the pan with the lime wedges for squeezing over.

Lean meat, fish, poultry, eggs, tofu: **1**
Breads, cereals, legumes, starchy
    vegetables: **1**
Dairy and dairy alternatives: **0**
Low–moderate carb vegetables: **2.5**
Healthy fats: **2**

# CHICKEN AND GREEN OLIVE COUSCOUS SALAD

20 G CARB PER SERVE

🍴 **Serves 4**   🕐 **Preparation: 15 minutes**
🎚 **Cooking: 10 minutes**   🎩 **Difficulty: Low**

1 tablespoon olive oil
1 tablespoon sweet paprika
400 g lean chicken breast fillet stir-fry
    strips, seasoned with pepper
½ cup (80 g) wholemeal couscous
½ cup (125 ml) salt-reduced chicken
    stock, heated
80 g pitted green olives, quartered
2 large Lebanese cucumbers, chopped
1 small red capsicum,
    seeded and chopped
2 spring onions, thinly sliced
150 g baby rocket leaves

Heat a large chargrill pan over medium–high heat.

Place the oil, paprika and chicken in a bowl, season with
freshly ground black pepper and toss well to coat. Chargrill
for 2–3 minutes each side or until golden and cooked through.
Transfer to a plate.

Meanwhile, place the couscous and hot stock in a heatproof bowl,
season with freshly ground black pepper and stir well. Stand,
covered, for 5 minutes or until the stock has been absorbed.
Using a fork, fluff the couscous to separate the grains.

Add the olives, cucumber, capsicum, spring onion, rocket and
paprika chicken to the couscous mixture and toss well to
combine. Serve warm, or cool before storing in an airtight
container in the fridge.

Note: The salad will keep for up to 2 days in the fridge.

# TUNA PESTO PASTA SALAD

**UNITS PER SERVE**

Lean meat, fish, poultry, eggs, tofu: **1**
Breads, cereals, legumes, starchy
    vegetables: **1**
Dairy and dairy alternatives: **1**
Low–moderate carb vegetables: **1.5**
Healthy fats: **2**

🍴 **Serves 4**  🕐 **Preparation: 15 minutes**
〰 **Cooking: 10 minutes**  🍳 **Difficulty: Low**

120 g dried low-GI or wholemeal
    spaghetti, broken into
    3–4 cm lengths
2 zucchini, halved lengthways
    and sliced
1 bunch broccolini, trimmed,
    stalks halved
400 g drained tinned tuna
    in springwater (see note)
2 tablespoons fresh basil pesto
finely grated zest and juice of 1 lemon
100 g parmesan, grated
250 g cherry tomatoes, halved

Cook the spaghetti in a large saucepan of boiling water for
6 minutes. Add the zucchini and broccolini and cook for a further
2 minutes. Drain, reserving ½ cup (125 ml) of the cooking water.
Transfer to a large bowl.

Add the remaining ingredients to the bowl and toss to combine,
adding some of the reserved cooking water to loosen if needed.
Season with freshly ground black pepper and serve warm.

Note: Because you will be draining off quite a bit of liquid, you will
need 2 x 425 g tins of tuna to have the required quantity for this
recipe. Store the leftover tuna in an airtight container in the fridge
for up to 3 days.

Lean meat, fish, poultry, eggs, tofu: **1**

Breads, cereals, legumes, starchy
vegetables: **1**

Dairy and dairy alternatives: **0.5**

Low–moderate carb vegetables: **1**

Healthy fats: **2.5**

# CHICKEN TIKKA AND SWEET POTATO LETTUCE CUPS

20 G CARB PER SERVE

🍴 **Serves 4**    🕐 **Preparation: 15 minutes**
🍲 **Cooking: 20 minutes**    🍳 **Difficulty: Low**

400 g lean chicken tenderloins,
seasoned with pepper

2 tablespoons tikka curry paste

200 g reduced-fat natural yoghurt

400 g peeled orange sweet potato,
very thinly sliced with a mandolin

8 iceberg lettuce leaves

2 Lebanese cucumbers, halved
lengthways and thinly sliced
diagonally

½ cup small mint leaves

20 g slivered almonds, toasted and
chopped

Combine the chicken, curry paste and half the yoghurt in a bowl.

Heat a large chargrill pan over high heat. Add half the sweet potato and cook, turning occasionally, for 4 minutes or until golden and just tender. Transfer to a plate and repeat with the remaining sweet potato.

Chargrill the chicken for 8–10 minutes, turning occasionally, until golden and cooked through. Transfer to a chopping board.

Divide the lettuce leaves among serving plates and fill with the sweet potato and cucumber. Slice the chicken and arrange over the top, then spoon over the remaining yoghurt. Sprinkle with the mint leaves and almonds and serve warm.

Lean meat, fish, poultry, eggs, tofu: **1**

Breads, cereals, legumes, starchy vegetables: **1**

Dairy and dairy alternatives: **0**

Low–moderate carb vegetables: **2**

Healthy fats: **0**

# VEGETABLE AND LENTIL TABBOULEH

🍴 **Serves 4**  🕐 **Preparation: 20 minutes**
🍲 **Cooking: 5 minutes**  🍳 **Difficulty: Low**

---

400 g firm tofu, sliced

4 zucchini, thinly sliced diagonally

640 g fresh vegetable and lentil salad

250 g cherry tomatoes, halved

1 small bunch flat-leaf parsley, stems and leaves finely chopped

¼ cup (60 ml) fat-free Italian dressing

Preheat the chargrill plate on a barbecue to medium–high. Add the tofu and zucchini and cook, turning occasionally, for 5 minutes or until golden and just cooked. Transfer to a large bowl.

Add the remaining ingredients and toss to combine. Season with freshly ground black pepper and serve.

# SPEEDY FISH PIE

**UNITS PER SERVE**
Lean meat, fish, poultry, eggs, tofu: **1**
Breads, cereals, legumes, starchy
   vegetables: **1**
Dairy and dairy alternatives: **1**
Low–moderate carb vegetables: **1**
Healthy fats: **0**

(fork) **Serves 4**   (clock) **Preparation: 15 minutes**
(pot) **Cooking: 20 minutes**   (difficulty) **Difficulty: Medium**

½ cup (80 g) wholemeal couscous
½ cup (125 ml) salt-reduced chicken
   stock, heated
2 tablespoons finely chopped chives
400 g skinless, boneless white fish
   fillets, chopped
2 tablespoons fresh Italian spice paste
100 g reduced-fat cream cheese,
   broken into pieces
1 cup (150 g) frozen peas,
   corn and carrot
200 g baby spinach leaves
lemon wedges, to serve

Preheat the oven to 220°C (200°C fan-forced).

Place the couscous and hot stock in a heatproof bowl, season with freshly ground black pepper and stir well. Stand, covered, for 5 minutes or until the stock has been completely absorbed. Using a fork, fluff the couscous to separate the grains. Stir in the chives.

Combine the fish, spice paste, cream cheese, frozen veggies and spinach in a 5 cm deep rectangular baking dish. Sprinkle the couscous mixture over the top and bake for 20 minutes or until golden and cooked through. Serve with the lemon wedges on the side.

Lean meat, fish, poultry, eggs, tofu: **1**

Breads, cereals, legumes, starchy
vegetables: **0**

Dairy and dairy alternatives: **1**

Low–moderate carb vegetables: **3**

Healthy fats: **0**

---

1 x 400 g tin chopped tomatoes

1 tablespoon salt-reduced tomato paste

¼ cup (60 g) fresh Italian spice paste

400 g drained, rinsed tinned
four-bean mix (see note)

2 cups (500 ml) salt-reduced
vegetable stock

4 small zucchini, spiralised

2 carrots, spiralised

100 g baby bocconcini, torn

½ cup basil leaves

# FOUR-BEAN BOLOGNESE

22 G CARB PER SERVE

🍽 **Serves 4**   🕐 **Preparation: 20 minutes**
🍲 **Cooking: 15 minutes**   🍳 **Difficulty: Low**

COOKS IN **UNDER 15 MINS**

Combine the tomatoes, tomato paste, spice paste, beans and stock in a large saucepan over medium heat. Bring to a simmer and cook for 15 minutes or until reduced and thickened.

Combine the zucchini and carrot in a bowl, season with freshly ground black pepper and toss well, then divide evenly among four serving bowls.

Spoon the sauce over the veggies and top with the bocconcini. Sprinkle with the basil leaves and serve.

**Note:** Because you will be draining off quite a bit of liquid, you will need 2 x 420 g tins of beans to have the required quantity for this recipe. Store the leftover bean mix in an airtight container in the fridge for up to 3 days.

# EGG SALAD WITH FETA DRESSING

🍽 **Serves 4**    🕐 **Preparation: 20 minutes**
🍳 **Cooking: 10 minutes**    🍲 **Difficulty: Medium**

**COOKS IN UNDER 10 MINS**

400 g small baby potatoes

300 g broccoli florets

300 g cauliflower florets

8 x 55 g eggs

2 cups baby rocket leaves

80 g pecans, toasted and broken

**FETA DRESSING**

200 g reduced-fat natural yoghurt

40 g reduced-fat Greek feta, crumbled

¼ cup (60 ml) fat-free French dressing

To make the feta dressing, combine all the ingredients in
a large bowl and season with freshly ground black pepper.

Cook the potatoes in a large saucepan of boiling water for
8–10 minutes or until just tender. Add the broccoli and cauliflower
and stir well, then drain. Halve the potatoes, then transfer all
the vegetables to the bowl and toss to coat in the dressing.

Meanwhile, cook the eggs in a separate saucepan of boiling water
for 5 minutes or until soft boiled. Drain, then carefully peel under
cold running water.

Add the rocket and pecans to the salad bowl and gently toss to
combine. Divide the salad among serving plates. Cut the warm
eggs in half lengthways and rest on top. Season with freshly ground
black pepper and serve warm.

**Note:** If you find the feta dressing is a little thick for your liking, add
more of the French dressing to taste or a few splashes of water to
reach your preferred consistency.

Lean meat, fish, poultry, eggs, tofu: **1**
Breads, cereals, legumes, starchy
   vegetables: **1**
Dairy and dairy alternatives: **0**
Low–moderate carb vegetables: **2**
Healthy fats: **2**

# CHICKEN CHOW MEIN

🍴 **Serves 4**   🕐 **Preparation: 10 minutes**
〰 **Cooking: 15 minutes**   🍲 **Difficulty: Low**

80 g dried brown rice noodles
400 g lean chicken breast fillet stir-fry
   strips, seasoned with pepper
2 tablespoons sunflower oil
1 tablespoon curry powder
¼ cup (60 ml) hoisin sauce
850 g frozen stir-fry Chinese
   vegetables

Place the noodles in a heatproof bowl and cover with boiling water. Stand for 5 minutes or until softened, then drain well and return to the bowl.

Heat a large non-stick wok over high heat. Combine the chicken, oil and curry powder in a bowl, then add half to the wok and stir-fry, tossing constantly, for 4 minutes or until golden and cooked. Transfer to the bowl with the noodles and toss together, then repeat with the remaining chicken.

Add the hoisin sauce and vegetables to the wok and stir-fry for 3 minutes. Return the chicken and noodle mixture to the wok and stir-fry for 1–2 minutes or until heated through and well combined. Serve hot.

**Note:** To reduce your total carbohydrate intake further, swap out the rice noodles for spiralised zucchini noodles.

Lean meat, fish, poultry, eggs, tofu: **1**
Breads, cereals, legumes, starchy
    vegetables: **1**
Dairy and dairy alternatives: **2**
Low–moderate carb vegetables: **1**
Healthy fats: **2**

# RAINBOW SALMON MACARONI WITH RICOTTA

🍴 **Serves 4**   🕐 **Preparation: 15 minutes**
🍲 **Cooking: 10 minutes**   🍳 **Difficulty: Low**

120 g small dried low-GI or
    wholemeal elbow macaroni
400 g drained tinned red salmon,
    broken into chunks (see note)
2 tablespoons chilli and garlic pesto
1 x 375 g packet simply stir-fry
    rainbow vegetables
440 g reduced-fat fresh ricotta
finely grated zest and juice of
    1 large lemon

Cook the macaroni in a large saucepan of boiling water for
8–10 minutes or until just tender. Drain, reserving ½ cup (125 ml)
of the cooking water. Transfer to a large bowl.

Add the remaining ingredients and gently toss to combine, adding
a little of the reserved cooking water to loosen if needed. Season
with freshly ground black pepper and serve.

Note: Because you will be draining off quite a bit of liquid, you will
need two 415 g tins of salmon to have the required quantity for this
recipe. Store the leftover salmon in an airtight container in the
fridge for up to 3 days.

# PRAWN AND SUMMER VEGGIE LASAGNE STACK

**UNITS PER SERVE**

Lean meat, fish, poultry, eggs, tofu: **1**

Breads, cereals, legumes, starchy
   vegetables: **1**

Dairy and dairy alternatives: **0**

Low–moderate carb vegetables: **4**

Healthy fats: **2**

---

🍴 Serves 4    🕐 Preparation: 20 minutes
🌀 Cooking: 20 minutes    👨‍🍳 Difficulty: Medium

---

400 g peeled and deveined cooked
   prawns, halved lengthways

4 tomatoes, sliced

1 bunch small radishes, trimmed and
   very thinly sliced into rounds

120 g dried low-GI or wholemeal
   lasagne sheets

300 g bought oil-free chargrilled
   eggplant slices

2 cups watercress sprigs

1 cup large basil leaves, plus extra small
   sprigs to serve

40 g pine nuts, toasted

**DRESSING**

finely grated zest and juice of 2 lemons

1 long red chilli, seeded and
   finely chopped

3 teaspoons fresh Italian herb paste

1 tablespoon extra virgin olive oil

To make the dressing, whisk together all the ingredients in a large bowl. Season with freshly ground black pepper.

Add the prawns, tomato and radish to the dressing and gently toss to coat. Set aside.

Bring a large saucepan of water to the boil. Add half the lasagne sheets and cook for 6–8 minutes or until just cooked. Using tongs, carefully remove each sheet and place side by side on trays lined with baking paper, making sure they don't overlap. Repeat with the remaining lasagne sheets.

Divide one-third of the prawn mixture among four serving plates, top with a lasagne sheet, half the eggplant slices, half the watercress and half the basil. Spoon over half the remaining prawn mixture, then top with the remaining lasagne sheets, eggplant, watercress and basil. Spoon over the remaining prawn mixture, sprinkle with the pine nuts and serve.

Lean meat, fish, poultry, eggs, tofu: **1**
Breads, cereals, legumes, starchy
  vegetables: **1**
Dairy and dairy alternatives: **1**
Low–moderate carb vegetables: **1.5**
Healthy fats: **1**

# ANTIPASTO CHICKEN PASTA

🍴 Serves 4    🕐 Preparation: 10 minutes
🍲 Cooking: 15 minutes    ⑨ Difficulty: Low

120 g small dried low-GI or
  wholemeal pasta shells
400 g lean chicken breast fillet, diced
  and seasoned with pepper
1 x 120 g packet chopped
  mixed kale mix
100 g mixed Tuscan antipasto,
  roughly chopped
100 g baby bocconcini, torn
1 cup small basil leaves

Cook the pasta in a large saucepan of boiling water for 8–10 minutes or until just tender. Drain, reserving ½ cup (125 ml) of the cooking water.

Meanwhile, heat a large, deep non-stick frying pan over high heat. Add the chicken and cook, stirring occasionally, for 8–10 minutes or until golden and cooked through.

Add the kale mix and antipasto to the chicken and cook, tossing, for 1–2 minutes or until the kale starts to wilt, adding a little of the reserved cooking water if needed to loosen. Divide the mixture among pasta bowls, top with the bocconcini and basil and serve.

Lean meat, fish, poultry, eggs, tofu: **1**
Breads, cereals, legumes, starchy
  vegetables: **1**
Dairy and dairy alternatives: **0**
Low–moderate carb vegetables: **1**
Healthy fats: **1**

# THAI TOFU AND RICE SALAD

🍴 **Serves 4**   🕐 **Preparation: 15 minutes**
🍲 **Cooking: 15 minutes**   👨‍🍳 **Difficulty: Low**

80 g Doongara (low-GI) clever
  white rice
¼ cup (60 g) fresh Thai herb paste
400 g firm tofu, cut into 2 cm pieces
2 x 250 g packets superfood
  vegetables stir-fry mix
finely grated zest and juice
  of 2 large limes
¼ cup (40 g) cashews,
  toasted and finely chopped

Cook the rice in boiling water for 12–15 minutes or until just tender. Drain and rinse under cold running water to cool.

Meanwhile, heat a large non-stick wok over high heat. Add the herb paste and tofu and stir-fry for 2 minutes. Add the vegetables and stir-fry for 3–5 minutes or until golden and heated through.

Remove the wok from the heat. Add the rice, lime zest and juice and cashews and toss to combine, then serve.

Lean meat, fish, poultry, eggs, tofu: **1**
Breads, cereals, legumes, starchy
   vegetables: **1**
Dairy and dairy alternatives: **1**
Low–moderate carb vegetables: **1**
Healthy fats: **2**

# VEGETABLE FRYING-PAN PIE

🍴 **Serves 4**   🕐 **Preparation: 15 minutes**
🍳 **Cooking: 20 minutes**   🍲 **Difficulty: Medium**

2 tablespoons olive oil
1 x 400 g packet traditional
   vegetables stir-fry mix
8 x 55 g eggs
200 ml low-fat milk
4 x 35 g slices multigrain bread,
   cut into 2 cm pieces
60 g aged cheddar, crumbled

Heat the oil in a large, deep frying pan with a flameproof handle over high heat. Add the vegetables and cook, stirring occasionally, for 5 minutes or until golden and heated through.

Whisk together the eggs and milk and season with freshly ground black pepper. Pour over the vegetables in the pan. Reduce the heat to medium–low and cook, stirring gently, for 2 minutes, then leave to cook untouched for 8 minutes or until the egg has set but is still a little wet on top.

Preheat the oven grill to high.

Combine the bread and cheddar in a bowl, then sprinkle over the egg mixture. Place under the grill for 3–5 minutes or until the egg is set and the top is golden and crispy. Take to the table and serve straight from the pan.

**UNITS PER SERVE**

Lean meat, fish, poultry, eggs, tofu: **1**

Breads, cereals, legumes, starchy
  vegetables: **1**

Dairy and dairy alternatives: **0**

Low–moderate carb vegetables: **2**

Healthy fats: **0**

**Serves 4**   **Preparation: 15 minutes**
**Cooking: 10 minutes**   **Difficulty: Medium**

2 teaspoons Mexican chilli powder

400 g skinless, boneless flathead fillets

1 x 400 g packet simply simmer
  veggie mix

1 x 300 g jar mild chunky tomato salsa

2 cups baby spinach leaves

2 x 70 g (small) wholemeal
  pita breads, torn

Heat a large, deep non-stick frying pan over medium–high heat. Sprinkle the chilli powder evenly over the flathead to coat on both sides. Add to the pan and cook for 3 minutes each side or until golden and almost cooked through. Transfer to a plate.

Add the veggie mix, salsa and spinach to the pan and cook, stirring occasionally, for 2–3 minutes or until the vegetables are heated through and the sauce has thickened slightly.

Return the flathead to the pan and simmer for 2 minutes or until the fish flakes easily when tested with a fork. Serve immediately with the pita bread alongside.

Note: You can replace the Mexican chilli powder with sweet paprika, if preferred.

Lean meat, fish, poultry, eggs, tofu: **1**
Breads, cereals, legumes, starchy
    vegetables: **1**
Dairy and dairy alternatives: **1**
Low–moderate carb vegetables: **1.5**
Healthy fats: **0**

# CHICKEN CAESAR BURGER

🍽 **Serves 4**   🕐 **Preparation: 10 minutes**
🍲 **Cooking: 20 minutes**   🍔 **Difficulty: Low**

**COOKS IN UNDER 20 MINS**

400 g lean uncrumbed chicken
    breast schnitzel steaks,
    seasoned with pepper
1 x 300 g packet mixed leaf iceberg
    lettuce blend
⅓ cup (80 ml) fat-free caesar dressing
4 x 40 g mixed seed and grain
    sandwich thins, split and toasted
4 tomatoes, sliced
80 g parmesan, shaved

Heat a large non-stick frying pan over high heat. Add half the chicken and cook, turning occasionally, for 8 minutes or until golden and cooked through. Transfer to a plate and repeat with the remaining chicken.

Combine the lettuce blend and dressing in a bowl.

Place the sandwich bases on serving plates and top with the tomato and half the salad. Add the warm chicken, parmesan and remaining salad, then finish with the sandwich tops. Secure with a large toothpick if needed and serve.

# CHICKEN PITA WITH ZUCCHINI SALAD

**UNITS PER SERVE**

Lean meat, fish, poultry, eggs, tofu: **1**

Breads, cereals, legumes, starchy
 vegetables: **1**

Dairy and dairy alternatives: **0**

Low–moderate carb vegetables: **2.5**

Healthy fats: **1**

---

400 g lean chicken tenderloins, sliced

3 teaspoons dried Moroccan seasoning

2 x 70 g (small) wholemeal
 pita breads, split

⅓ cup (80 g) hummus

1½ cups mixed salad leaves
 (baby rocket, baby spinach,
 shredded red radicchio)

**ZUCCHINI SALAD**

4 zucchini, spiralised

2 spring onions, thinly sliced

⅓ cup (80 g) whole-egg mayonnaise

finely grated zest and juice of 1 lemon

½ cup small mint leaves

½ cup small coriander leaves

**Serves 4**   **Preparation: 15 minutes**
**Cooking: 10 minutes**   **Difficulty: Low**

COOKS IN **UNDER 10 MINS**

To make the zucchini salad, combine all the ingredients in a bowl and season with freshly ground black pepper.

Preheat a large chargrill pan over high heat. Combine the chicken and Moroccan seasoning, then add to the pan and cook, turning occasionally, for 8 minutes or until golden and cooked through. Transfer to a plate.

Place a pita round on each serving plate and spread with the hummus. Top with the salad leaves, zucchini salad and warm chicken, then wrap up and eat.

soups & salads

## UNITS PER SERVE

Lean meat, fish, poultry, eggs, tofu: **1**
Breads, cereals, legumes, starchy
    vegetables: **1**
Dairy and dairy alternatives: **0**
Low–moderate carb vegetables: **2.5**
Healthy fats: **1**

# TUSCAN PORK AND QUINOA SALAD

16 G CARB PER SERVE

ONLY **6** INGREDIENTS

🍴 **Serves 4**   🕐 **Preparation: 15 minutes**
🍳 **Cooking: 15 minutes**   🍲 **Difficulty: Low**

80 g quinoa, rinsed well
2 bunches asparagus
400 g trimmed lean pork fillet,
    seasoned with pepper
100 g drained Tuscan antipasto mix
2 cups leafy green salad mix
finely grated zest and juice of 1 lemon

Cook the quinoa in a saucepan of boiling water for 12 minutes until just tender. Add the asparagus to another saucepan of boiling water and cook for 2–3 minutes until just tender, then drain. Transfer the quinoa and asparagus to a large bowl.

Meanwhile, heat a large non-stick frying pan over high heat. Add half the pork and cook, turning occasionally, for 5 minutes or until golden and cooked. Transfer to the bowl and gently toss to combine, then repeat with the remaining pork.

Add the remaining ingredients and toss to combine. Serve warm.

# CHICKEN AND ZUCCHINI CAPRESE SALAD

18 G CARB PER SERVE

**Serves 4**    **Preparation: 15 minutes**
**Cooking: 20 minutes**    **Difficulty: Low**

**UNITS PER SERVE**
Lean meat, fish, poultry, eggs, tofu: **1**
Breads, cereals, legumes, starchy
    vegetables: **0.5**
Dairy and dairy alternatives: **1**
Low–moderate carb vegetables: **2.5**
Healthy fats: **2**

4 zucchini, thinly sliced lengthways
400 g lean chicken tenderloins, halved
    lengthways, seasoned with pepper
6 tomatoes, thinly sliced into rounds
100 g baby bocconcini, torn
1 cup small basil leaves
2 x 35 g slices multigrain sourdough
    bread, toasted and halved

**DRESSING**
2 tablespoons extra virgin olive oil
⅓ cup (80 ml) balsamic vinegar

To make the dressing, whisk together all the ingredients in a jug. Season with freshly ground black pepper.

Heat a large chargrill pan over high heat. Add half the zucchini and cook, turning occasionally, for 4 minutes or until golden and cooked. Transfer to a plate and repeat with the remaining zucchini. Add the chicken to the pan and cook, turning occasionally, for 8 minutes or until golden and cooked through. Transfer to the plate.

Evenly layer the zucchini, tomato, chicken, bocconcini and basil on serving plates and drizzle with the dressing. Season with freshly ground black pepper and serve warm with the toast.

**9 G CARB PER SERVE**

**UNITS PER SERVE**

Lean meat, fish, poultry, eggs, tofu: **1**

Breads, cereals, legumes, starchy
vegetables: **0.5**

Dairy and dairy alternatives: **1**

Low–moderate carb vegetables: **1.5**

Healthy fats: **3**

# CURRIED CHICKPEA AND CHICKEN SALAD

Serves 4    Preparation: 15 minutes
Cooking: 15 minutes    Difficulty: Low

COOKS IN **UNDER 15 MINS**

2 tablespoons olive oil

160 g drained, rinsed tinned chickpeas
(see note)

400 g lean chicken breast, diced and
seasoned with pepper

1 leek, white part only, thinly sliced

1 tablespoon curry powder

80 g haloumi, chopped

1 small iceberg lettuce, chopped

40 g slivered almonds, toasted
and chopped

mint leaves and lime wedges, to serve

Heat the oil in a large, deep non-stick frying pan over high heat. Add the chickpeas, chicken, leek and curry powder and cook, stirring occasionally, for 10 minutes or until golden and the chicken is cooked. Add the haloumi and cook, stirring constantly, for 2 minutes or until golden and heated through.

Divide the lettuce among serving bowls, top with the chicken mixture and sprinkle with the almonds. Garnish with the mint leaves and serve with the lime wedges.

Note: Because you will be draining off quite a bit of liquid, you will need a 400 g tin of chickpeas to have the required quantity for this recipe. Store the leftover chickpeas in an airtight container in the fridge for up to 3 days.

# CHICKEN NOODLE SOUP

**UNITS PER SERVE**

Lean meat, fish, poultry, eggs, tofu: **1**

Breads, cereals, legumes, starchy
vegetables: **1**

Dairy and dairy alternatives: **0**

Low–moderate carb vegetables: **1**

Healthy fats: **2**

---

🍴 **Serves 4**   🕐 **Preparation: 10 minutes**
🥘 **Cooking: 15 minutes**   🎩 **Difficulty: Low**

COOKS IN **UNDER 15 MINS**

400 g lean chicken tenderloins, sliced
and seasoned with pepper

1 cup (150 g) frozen peas, corn and
carrot mix

1 litre salt-reduced chicken stock

80 g rice vermicelli, broken into pieces

120 g baby spinach leaves

¼ cup (60 g) fresh basil pesto

Combine all the ingredients in a large saucepan and bring to the boil over high heat. Reduce the heat and simmer, stirring occasionally, for 15 minutes or until the chicken is cooked through.

Divide among bowls and serve hot.

Lean meat, fish, poultry, eggs, tofu: **1**

Breads, cereals, legumes, starchy
   vegetables: **1**

Dairy and dairy alternatives: **0**

Low–moderate carb vegetables: **1.5**

Healthy fats: **0.5**

# CRISPY TOFU AND GINGER SOBA NOODLE SOUP

**20 G CARB PER SERVE**

**ONLY 6 INGREDIENTS**

🍴 **Serves 4**   🕐 **Preparation: 15 minutes**
🍲 **Cooking: 10 minutes**   🎩 **Difficulty: Low**

2 teaspoons sesame oil

400 g firm tofu, cut into 1 cm pieces,
   patted dry with paper towel and
   seasoned with pepper

1 litre salt-reduced vegetable stock

5 cm piece ginger, cut into thin
   matchsticks

100 g shelf-fresh soba noodles

2 bunches (6 pieces) baby bok choy,
   leaves separated

Heat the oil in a large non-stick wok over high heat. Add the tofu and stir-fry for 4 minutes or until very golden and crispy. Transfer to a plate.

Add all the remaining ingredients to the wok and boil, stirring occasionally, for 5 minutes or until the noodles are just tender and the bok choy has wilted. Divide among bowls, top with the crispy tofu and serve hot.

# HEARTY FISH SOUP

24 G CARB PER SERVE

🍴 **Serves 4**  🕐 **Preparation: 20 minutes**
〰 **Cooking: 20 minutes**  👩‍🍳 **Difficulty: Low**

2 tablespoons olive oil

1 red onion, chopped

2 zucchini, chopped

2 sticks celery, chopped

2 carrots, chopped

2 teaspoons dried Italian herbs

1 x 410 g tin rich and thick basil and garlic chopped tomatoes

1 litre salt-reduced chicken stock

120 g dried low-GI or wholemeal spaghetti, broken into pieces

400 g skinless, boneless snapper fillets, cut into 3 cm pieces

1 cup basil leaves

Heat the oil in a large saucepan over high heat. Add the onion, zucchini, celery, carrot, dried herbs and tomatoes and cook, stirring constantly, for 10 minutes or until softened.

Add the stock and spaghetti to the saucepan and cook, stirring occasionally, for 5 minutes. Add the fish and cook, stirring once, for 5 minutes or until the spaghetti and fish are cooked.

Divide among bowls and season with freshly ground black pepper. Sprinkle with the basil and serve.

**UNITS PER SERVE**

Lean meat, fish, poultry, eggs, tofu: **1**

Breads, cereals, legumes, starchy
  vegetables: **0.5**

Dairy and dairy alternatives: **1**

Low–moderate carb vegetables: **1**

Healthy fats: **3**

# TOMATO AND CHICKEN SALAD WITH AVO TOASTS

11 G CARB PER SERVE

(🍽) **Serves 4**   (🕐) **Preparation: 15 minutes, plus 5 minutes standing time**
(🍳) **Cooking: 10 minutes**   (👩‍🍳) **Difficulty: Low**

COOKS IN **UNDER 10 MINS**

1 tablespoon olive oil

400 g lean chicken breast strips,
  seasoned with pepper

1 teaspoon fresh garlic paste

4 tomatoes, sliced

1 tablespoon extra virgin olive oil

2 tablespoons red wine vinegar

80 g avocado

2 x 35 g slices multigrain
  sourdough bread, toasted

¼ cup chopped basil, plus extra
  small leaves to serve

2 cups mixed salad leaves

80 g parmesan, shaved

Heat the olive oil in a large non-stick frying pan over high heat. Add the chicken and garlic and cook, stirring occasionally, for 10 minutes or until golden and cooked through.

Meanwhile, combine the tomato, extra virgin olive oil and vinegar in a large bowl and season with freshly ground black pepper.

Add the chicken to the tomato mixture and gently toss to combine. Stand for 5 minutes.

Mash the avocado over the toast, then cut each piece into quarters.

Add the basil, salad leaves and parmesan to the chicken mixture and gently toss together. Divide among bowls and serve with the avocado toast.

# NO-COOK THAI TOFU SALAD

Serves 4  Preparation: 20 minutes
Difficulty: Low

**NO COOKING REQUIRED**

**UNITS PER SERVE**

Lean meat, fish, poultry, eggs, tofu: **1**
Breads, cereals, legumes, starchy
   vegetables: **1**
Dairy and dairy alternatives: **0**
Low–moderate carb vegetables: **1.5**
Healthy fats: **1**

80 g rice vermicelli
400 g firm tofu, cut into 1 cm pieces
1 long red chilli, finely chopped
finely grated zest and juice of 2 limes
1 cup bean sprouts
2 x 315 g Thai salad kits
   (including fried shallot but
   discarding dressing sachet)

Place the noodles in a heatproof bowl and cover with boiling water. Stand for 5 minutes or until softened. Drain well, then return to the bowl.

Add all the remaining ingredients to the bowl and toss well to combine. Season with freshly ground pepper and serve.

## UNITS PER SERVE

Lean meat, fish, poultry, eggs, tofu: **1.5**
Breads, cereals, legumes, starchy
    vegetables: **0**
Dairy and dairy alternatives: **0.5**
Low–moderate carb vegetables: **3**
Healthy fats: **2**

# BEEF SALAD WITH CHILLI YOGHURT

11 G
CARB PER
SERVE

Serves 4   Preparation: 20 minutes
Cooking: 10 minutes   Difficulty: Low

4 x 150 g lean beef eye fillet steaks,
    seasoned with pepper
4 tomatoes, chopped
2 Lebanese cucumbers, chopped
300 g brussels sprouts, finely shredded
4 spring onions, chopped
160 g avocado, chopped
1 small bunch coriander, leaves picked
finely grated zest and juice of 2 limes

### CHILLI YOGHURT

1 teaspoon fresh garlic paste
1 long red chilli, seeded and
    finely chopped
200 g reduced-fat natural yoghurt
2 teaspoons fish sauce

To make the chilli yoghurt, whisk together all the ingredients in a small bowl.

Heat a large non-stick frying pan over high heat. Add the steaks and cook for 3 minutes each side for medium, or until cooked to your liking. Transfer to a plate.

Combine all the remaining ingredients in a bowl, then divide among serving plates. Top with the steaks and serve hot, drizzled with the chilli yoghurt.

# GREEK CHICKEN SALAD

**9 G CARB PER SERVE**

Lean meat, fish, poultry, eggs, tofu: **1.5**

Breads, cereals, legumes, starchy vegetables: **0**

Dairy and dairy alternatives: **0.5**

Low–moderate carb vegetables: **2.5**

Healthy fats: **1.5**

Serves 4   Preparation: 15 minutes
Cooking: 20 minutes   Difficulty: Low

---

600 g lean chicken breast strips, seasoned with pepper

1 tablespoon olive oil

1 tablespoon dried oregano

2 teaspoons fresh garlic paste

1 small iceberg lettuce, chopped

4 tomatoes, cut into wedges

2 Lebanese cucumbers, chopped

80 g feta-stuffed green olives (approximately 40 g olives and 40 g feta)

1 small red onion, thinly sliced

½ cup (125 ml) fat-free, low-sugar Greek salad dressing

Heat a large chargrill pan over high heat. Combine the chicken, oil, oregano and garlic in a bowl. Add half the chicken to the pan and cook, turning occasionally, for 8 minutes or until golden and cooked through. Transfer to a plate, then repeat with the remaining chicken.

Meanwhile, combine all the remaining ingredients in a bowl, then divide among plates.

Arrange the chicken over the salad and serve hot.

**UNITS PER SERVE**

Lean meat, fish, poultry, eggs, tofu: **1.5**
Breads, cereals, legumes, starchy
   vegetables: **0**
Dairy and dairy alternatives: **0**
Low–moderate carb vegetables: **2**
Healthy fats: **4**

# CHICKEN SATAY SOUP

9 G CARB PER SERVE

🍴 **Serves 4**   🕐 **Preparation: 15 minutes**
♨ **Cooking: 15 minutes**   ⓢ **Difficulty: Low**

2 tablespoons yellow curry paste
600 g lean chicken tenderloins, sliced
1 red onion, halved and thinly sliced
2 tablespoons fresh almond butter
1.5 litres salt-reduced chicken stock
1 bunch Chinese broccoli,
   cut into 2 cm lengths
300 g snowpeas, trimmed
small coriander sprigs and lime wedges,
   to serve

Heat the curry paste in a large heavy-based saucepan over high heat. Add the chicken and onion and cook, stirring occasionally, for 10 minutes. Stir in the almond butter, then add the stock and bring to the boil.

Add the broccoli and snowpeas to the pan and boil for 1–2 minutes or until the greens are just cooked. Season with freshly ground black pepper.

Divide the soup among bowls, top with the coriander sprigs and serve with the lime wedges.

**UNITS PER SERVE**

Lean meat, fish, poultry, eggs, tofu: **1.5**

Breads, cereals, legumes, starchy
vegetables: **0**

Dairy and dairy alternatives: **0**

Low–moderate carb vegetables: **4**

Healthy fats: **2**

---

1 tablespoon sunflower oil

1 teaspoon Chinese five-spice powder

600 g lean chicken breast strips

4 spring onions, thinly sliced diagonally

300 g Chinese cabbage (wombok),
finely shredded

1 red capsicum, seeded and chopped

1 carrot, cut into thin matchsticks

40 g slivered almonds, toasted
and chopped

**DRESSING**

2 tablespoons salt-reduced soy sauce

juice of 1 lemon

½ teaspoon sesame oil

# CHINESE CABBAGE AND CHICKEN SALAD

**8 G CARB PER SERVE**

🍽 **Serves 4**   🕐 **Preparation: 20 minutes**
🍲 **Cooking: 5 minutes**   🎩 **Difficulty: Low**

COOKS IN **UNDER 5 MINS**

To make the dressing, whisk together all the ingredients in
a small bowl. Season with freshly ground black pepper.

Heat the oil in a large non-stick wok over high heat. Add the
five-spice powder, chicken and spring onion and stir-fry for
5 minutes or until golden and cooked through.

Combine the cabbage, capsicum, carrot and almonds in a large
bowl. Add the chicken mixture and dressing and toss well to
combine. Serve warm.

# PORTUGUESE CHICKEN SALAD

🍴 **Serves 4**   🕐 **Preparation: 20 minutes**
🍲 **Cooking: 15 minutes**   🍽 **Difficulty: Low**

COOKS IN **UNDER 15 MINS**

**UNITS PER SERVE**

Lean meat, fish, poultry, eggs, tofu: **1.5**
Breads, cereals, legumes, starchy
    vegetables: **0**
Dairy and dairy alternatives: **0**
Low-moderate carb vegetables: **2.5**
Healthy fats: **4**

4 x 150 g lean chicken breast fillets,
    scored and seasoned with pepper
2 tablespoons Portuguese seasoning
finely grated zest and juice of 2 lemons
2 tablespoons extra virgin olive oil
1 teaspoon dried oregano
120 g baby rocket leaves
500 g baby grape tomatoes, halved
1 small red onion, halved and
    thinly sliced
2 Lebanese cucumbers, peeled into
    long thin ribbons
80 g mixed pitted olives, halved

Preheat the chargrill plate on a barbecue to medium–high. Combine the chicken, seasoning and half the lemon zest and juice and season with freshly ground black pepper. Chargrill for 12–15 minutes or until dark golden and cooked through. Transfer to a board.

Whisk together the oil, oregano and remaining lemon zest and juice in a large bowl. Add the rocket, tomatoes, onion, cucumber and olives and gently toss together. Divide among serving plates.

Slice the chicken and arrange over the salad. Serve warm.

# PRAWN TOM YUM SOUP

**8 G CARB PER SERVE**

**UNITS PER SERVE**

Lean meat, fish, poultry, eggs, tofu: **1.5**

Breads, cereals, legumes, starchy
vegetables: **0**

Dairy and dairy alternatives: **0**

Low–moderate carb vegetables: **2**

Healthy fats: **2**

Serves 4    Preparation: 15 minutes
Cooking: 10 minutes    Difficulty: Low

2 tablespoons tom yum paste

600 g peeled, deveined small
raw prawns

1.5 litres salt-reduced chicken stock

4 kaffir lime leaves, torn

200 g fresh shiitake mushrooms, sliced

300 g oyster mushrooms, torn in half

150 g button mushrooms, halved

500 g cherry tomatoes, halved

120 g baby spinach leaves

sliced long red chilli, coriander leaves
and lime wedges, to serve

Heat the tom yum paste in a large saucepan over high heat. Add the prawns and cook, stirring constantly, for 1 minute.

Add the stock, lime leaves, mushrooms, tomatoes and spinach and bring to the boil. Cook, stirring occasionally, for 5 minutes or until the prawns are just cooked.

Divide the soup among bowls. Sprinkle with the chilli and coriander and serve with the lime wedges.

**UNITS PER SERVE**

Lean meat, fish, poultry, eggs, tofu: **1.5**
Breads, cereals, legumes, starchy
    vegetables: **0**
Dairy and dairy alternatives: **0**
Low–moderate carb vegetables: **2.5**
Healthy fats: **3**

# CAULIFLOWER CHOWDER WITH CRUNCHY TOPPED SALMON

10 G CARB PER SERVE

🍴 Serves 4  🕐 Preparation: 20 minutes
〰 Cooking: 15 minutes  👨‍🍳 Difficulty: Low

1 tablespoon olive oil
1 leek, white part only, sliced
1 teaspoon fresh garlic paste
4 zucchini, chopped
500 g cauliflower florets, chopped
1 litre salt-reduced chicken stock
1 tablespoon chilli and garlic pesto
80 g finely chopped mixed nuts (use
    pine nuts, brazil nuts and pecans)
4 x 150 g skinless, boneless
    salmon fillets
small flat-leaf parsley leaves and
    lemon wedges, to serve

Heat the oil in a large saucepan over high heat, add the leek, garlic paste and zucchini and cook, stirring occasionally, for 5 minutes. Add the cauliflower and stock. Bring to the boil and cook, stirring occasionally, for 10 minutes or until the vegetables are soft. Remove from the heat. Use a hand-held blender to blitz the soup until it is completely smooth.

Meanwhile, preheat the oven grill to high. Combine the pesto and nuts. Place the salmon on a non-stick baking tray and spread the tops with the pesto mixture. Season with freshly ground black pepper. Cook under the grill for 8 minutes or until the fish is cooked and the topping is golden.

Divide the soup among shallow bowls and place a piece of salmon in the centre. Sprinkle with the parsley and serve with the lemon wedges.

**8 G
CARB PER
SERVE**

# FISH AND SAMBAL BEAN SALAD

🍴 **Serves 4**   🕐 **Preparation: 20 minutes**
🍳 **Cooking: 10 minutes**   🍥 **Difficulty: Low**

COOKS IN **UNDER 10 MINS**

4 x 150 g skinless, boneless
  thick-cut barramundi fillets,
  seasoned with pepper
2 baby cos lettuces, leaves separated
1 cup bean sprouts

**SAMBAL BEAN SALAD**
450 g baby green beans, trimmed
1 tablespoon fresh red chilli paste
2 teaspoons fish sauce
finely grated zest and juice of
  2 large lemons
120 g blanched almonds, toasted and
  finely chopped
1 small bunch coriander, leaves picked,
  stems washed and finely chopped

To make the sambal bean salad, heat a large non-stick frying pan over high heat. Add the beans and ¼ cup (60 ml) water and cook, tossing, for 2 minutes or until just tender and the water has evaporated. Transfer to a bowl. Add the remaining ingredients and gently toss to combine.

Reheat the same pan over high heat. Add the barramundi and cook for 4 minutes each side or until golden and cooked through.

Divide the lettuce, bean sprouts and sambal bean salad among plates. Top with the barramundi, season with freshly ground black pepper and serve.

# DUKKAH-CRUSTED TOFU SALAD

**UNITS PER SERVE**

Lean meat, fish, poultry, eggs, tofu: **1.5**
Breads, cereals, legumes, starchy
   vegetables: **0**
Dairy and dairy alternatives: **0**
Low–moderate carb vegetables: **2.5**
Healthy fats: **2.5**

🍴 **Serves 4**   🕐 **Preparation: 15 minutes**
🍲 **Cooking: 10 minutes**   🥄 **Difficulty: Low**

COOKS IN **UNDER 10 MINS**

2 tablespoons (20 g) pistachio dukkah
600 g firm tofu, cut into 4 steaks
1 x 300 g packet rainbow coleslaw mix
300 g mixed salad leaves
½ cup small mint leaves
½ cup small coriander leaves
2 tablespoons fat-free
   coleslaw dressing
⅓ cup (80 g) whole-egg mayonnaise
⅓ cup (80 g) hummus

Preheat a large non-stick frying pan over medium–high heat. Sprinkle the dukkah over the tofu steaks, coating evenly on both sides. Add to the pan and cook for 3 minutes each side or until golden and heated through.

Meanwhile, combine the coleslaw mix, salad leaves, mint, coriander, dressing and mayonnaise in a bowl. Divide evenly among serving bowls. Place the tofu steaks on top of the salad and serve warm, topped with the hummus.

# VINDALOO LAMB AND COOLING SLAW

**UNITS PER SERVE**

Lean meat, fish, poultry, eggs, tofu: **1.5**
Breads, cereals, legumes, starchy
   vegetables: **0**
Dairy and dairy alternatives: **0.5**
Low–moderate carb vegetables: **2**
Healthy fats: **2**

🍴 Serves 4   🕐 Preparation: 15 minutes
〰 Cooking: 10 minutes   Difficulty: Low

600 g lean lamb backstrap
2 tablespoons vindaloo curry paste

**COOLING SLAW**
200 g reduced-fat natural yoghurt
finely grated zest and juice of 2 lemons
2 x 350 g kaleslaw kits (dressing
   sachets discarded)
1 small bunch mint, leaves picked

Heat a large chargrill pan over high heat. Coat the lamb all over with the curry paste, then add to the pan and cook for 4 minutes each side for medium, or until cooked to your liking. Transfer to a board.

To make the cooling slaw, whisk together the yoghurt and lemon zest and juice in a bowl. Add the slaw mix and mint and toss until well combined.

Divide the cooling slaw among plates. Slice the lamb diagonally and arrange next to the slaw. Serve hot.

**UNITS PER SERVE**

Lean meat, fish, poultry, eggs, tofu: **1.5**

Breads, cereals, legumes, starchy
vegetables: **0**

Dairy and dairy alternatives: **0**

Low–moderate carb vegetables: **2**

Healthy fats: **1**

# GARLIC AND HERB ROASTED CHICKEN SALAD

7 G
CARB PER
SERVE

ONLY
**6**
INGREDIENTS

🍽 **Serves 4** 🕐 **Preparation: 15 minutes**
🍳 **Cooking: 15 minutes** 🍲 **Difficulty: Low**

600 g lean chicken tenderloins,
halved diagonally

1 tablespoon onion, garlic and Italian
herb paste

1 bunch small radishes, trimmed and
very thinly sliced into rounds

4 Lebanese cucumbers, peeled into
long thin ribbons

1 x 160 g packet mixed leaf
rocket salad mix

½ cup (125 ml) fat-free Italian
salad dressing

Preheat the oven to 220°C (200°C fan-forced). Line a large baking tray with baking paper.

Coat the chicken in the herb paste and spread over the prepared tray. Season with freshly ground black pepper. Roast, turning once, for 15 minutes or until golden and cooked through. Transfer to a large bowl.

Add the remaining ingredients and gently toss to combine. Divide among plates and serve warm.

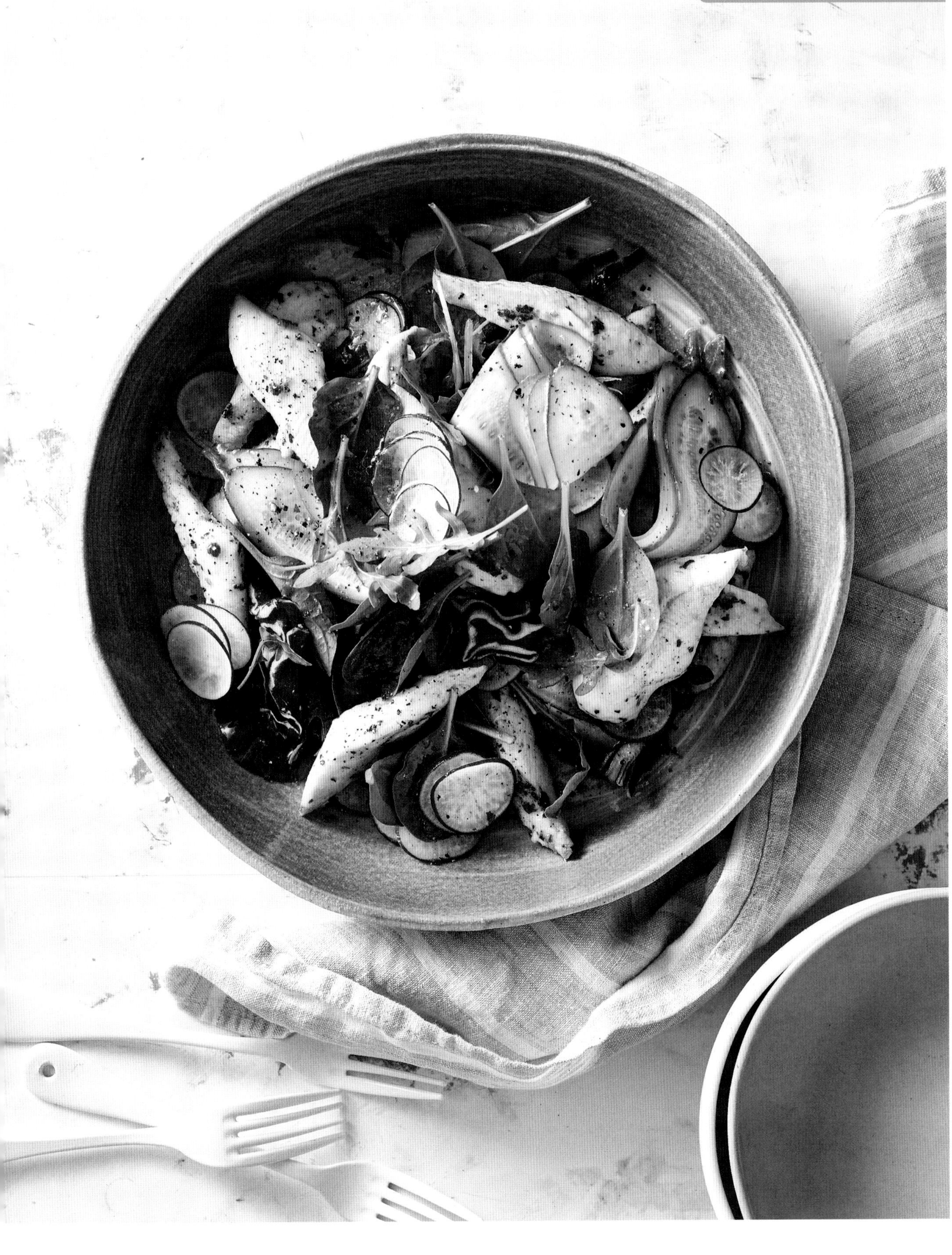

# PORK AND ZUCCHINI FAJITA

**UNITS PER SERVE**

Lean meat, fish, poultry, eggs, tofu: **1.5**

Breads, cereals, legumes, starchy
   vegetables: **0**

Dairy and dairy alternatives: **1**

Low–moderate carb vegetables: **2**

Healthy fats: **1**

🍴 Serves 4    🕐 Preparation: 15 minutes
♨ Cooking: 20 minutes    👨‍🍳 Difficulty: Low

2 x 250 g packets fresh
   zucchini spaghetti
2 x 125 g tins diced capsicum, drained
600 g lean pork stir-fry strips
1 x 40 g packet fajita spice mix
100 g mozzarella, grated
40 g unsalted shelled pistachios,
   finely chopped
small coriander sprigs and lime wedges,
   to serve

Preheat the oven to 220°C (200°C fan-forced).

Scatter the zucchini evenly over the base of a 5 cm deep,
rectangular baking dish. Sprinkle evenly with the capsicum.

Combine the pork and spice, then sprinkle over the capsicum. Top
evenly with mozzarella and bake for 20 minutes or until the cheese
is melted and golden.

Scatter with the pistachios and coriander sprigs and serve with the
lime wedges.

Lean meat, fish, poultry, eggs, tofu: **1.5**
Breads, cereals, legumes, starchy
   vegetables: **0**
Dairy and dairy alternatives: **0**
Low–moderate carb vegetables: **3.5**
Healthy fats: **2**

# BEEF WITH CAPSICUM SALSA

🍴 **Serves 4**   🕐 **Preparation: 15 minutes**
🍳 **Cooking: 15 minutes**   🥘 **Difficulty: Low**

600 g heart-smart beef, diced and
   seasoned with pepper
1 x 500 g packet 3 colour capsicums,
   thinly sliced
1 x 300 g jar chunky tomato salsa
300 g shredded iceberg lettuce
50 g baby rocket leaves
160 g avocado, sliced

Preheat a large non-stick frying pan over high heat. Cook the beef in three batches for 4 minutes each, tossing constantly, until well browned and cooked to medium. Transfer each batch to a bowl before adding the next.

Add the capsicum to the pan and cook, tossing constantly, for 2 minutes or until just tender and golden. Add the salsa and ⅓ cup (80 ml) water and stir well, then remove from the heat.

Divide the warm salsa mixture among plates and top with the beef. Serve with the lettuce, rocket and avocado alongside.

Lean meat, fish, poultry, eggs, tofu: **1.5**
Breads, cereals, legumes, starchy
   vegetables: **0**
Dairy and dairy alternatives: **0**
Low–moderate carb vegetables: **2**
Healthy fats: **2**

# EGGPLANT STEAKS WITH BEEF AND HUMMUS

8 G CARB PER SERVE

ONLY **6** INGREDIENTS

🍴 **Serves 4**   🕐 **Preparation: 15 minutes**
〽 **Cooking: 15 minutes**   🍲 **Difficulty: Low**

2 small (600 g) eggplants,
   cut into 1 cm thick slices
600 g lean beef strips,
   seasoned with pepper
⅓ cup (80 g) hummus
2 x 180 g packets mixed leaf baby
   leaves and beetroot
20 pitted kalamata olives
lemon wedges, to serve

Preheat a large chargrill pan over high heat. Add half the eggplant and cook for 2 minutes each side or until tender and golden. Transfer to a plate and repeat with the remaining eggplant.

Add half the beef to the pan and cook, turning constantly, for 2 minutes or until golden and cooked to medium. Transfer to a plate and repeat with the remaining beef.

Dollop some hummus onto each plate, then top with the mixed leaves, eggplant, beef and olives. Serve with the lemon wedges.

Lean meat, fish, poultry, eggs, tofu: **1.5**
Breads, cereals, legumes, starchy
  vegetables: **0**
Dairy and dairy alternatives: **0**
Low–moderate carb vegetables: **2**
Healthy fats: **1.5**

# ITALIAN BEEF AND CAULIFLOWER RICE TOSS

🍴 Serves 4    🕐 Preparation: 15 minutes
🍲 Cooking: 15 minutes    👩‍🍳 Difficulty: Low

600 g lean beef strips,
  seasoned with pepper
¼ cup (60 g) fresh Italian herb paste
1 tablespoon olive oil
1 x 500 g packet frozen cauliflower
  rice (treated as raw weight of
  150 g per unit)
1 x 150 g packet mixed salad, kale leaf
  and spinach
100 g mixed Tuscan antipasto,
  roughly chopped (see note)

Heat a large, deep non-stick frying pan over high heat. Combine the beef and herb paste, then cook the beef in three batches for 4 minutes each, tossing constantly, until well browned and cooked to medium. Transfer each batch to a bowl before adding the next.

Heat the oil in the pan and reduce the heat to medium. Add the cauliflower rice and cook, stirring constantly, for 1 minute. Add the mixed leaves, antipasto and ¼ cup (60 ml) water and cook, tossing, for 1–2 minutes or until the leaves are just wilted. Remove the pan from the heat.

Return the beef to the pan and toss gently to combine. Divide among plates and serve.

**Note:** Deli mixes can often vary, but on average this antipasto mix provides you with ½ unit healthy fats and ½ unit moderate–low carb veg per serve.

# WARM SALMON AND VEGETABLE SALAD WITH ITALIAN YOGHURT

**UNITS PER SERVE**

Lean meat, fish, poultry, eggs, tofu: **1.5**

Breads, cereals, legumes, starchy
vegetables: **0**

Dairy and dairy alternatives: **0.5**

Low–moderate carb vegetables: **1.5**

Healthy fats: **3**

Serves 4    Preparation: 10 minutes
Cooking: 5 minutes    Difficulty: Low

COOKS IN **UNDER 5 MINS**

1 tablespoon olive oil

1 x 450 g packet frozen broccoli,
carrot and cauliflower

2 cups baby rocket leaves

600 g drained tinned red salmon
(see note)

80 g blanched almonds, toasted
and chopped

**ITALIAN YOGHURT**

200 g reduced-fat natural yoghurt

¼ cup (60 g) fresh Italian herb paste

2 tablespoons white wine vinegar

To make the Italian yoghurt, combine all the ingredients in a bowl and season with freshly ground black pepper.

Heat the oil in a large non-stick frying pan over high heat. Add the frozen vegetables and cook, tossing constantly, for 5 minutes or until golden and heated through.

Divide the rocket among plates. Top with the vegetables, then the salmon and almonds, and serve with the Italian yoghurt.

**Note:** Because you will be draining off quite a bit of liquid, you will need two 415 g tins of salmon to have the required quantity for this recipe. Store the leftover salmon in an airtight container in the fridge for up to 3 days.

**UNITS PER SERVE**

Lean meat, fish, poultry, eggs, tofu: **1.5**

Breads, cereals, legumes, starchy
  vegetables: **0**

Dairy and dairy alternatives: **0.5**

Low–moderate carb vegetables: **1.5**

Healthy fats: **2**

---

2 tablespoons korma curry paste

600 g lean chicken breast, diced

2 cups (500 ml) salt-reduced
  chicken stock

1 x 450 g packet frozen broccoli,
  carrot and cauliflower

1 x 120 g packet baby spinach leaves

**YOGHURT DRIZZLE**

200 g reduced-fat natural yoghurt

2 teaspoons fresh coriander herb paste

1 teaspoon fresh basil herb paste

large pinch dried chilli flakes (optional)

# CHICKEN AND VEGETABLE KORMA

🍴 **Serves 4**   🕐 **Preparation: 15 minutes**
🍲 **Cooking: 15 minutes**   👩‍🍳 **Difficulty: Low**

COOKS IN **UNDER 15 MINS**

To make the yoghurt drizzle, whisk together all the ingredients
in a jug. Season with freshly ground black pepper.

Heat a large, deep non-stick frying pan over high heat. Add the
curry paste and chicken and cook, stirring constantly, for 2 minutes.
Add the stock and stir well, then bring to the boil and cook, stirring
occasionally, for 8 minutes or until reduced by half.

Add the frozen vegetables and spinach to the pan and stir well,
then boil for a further 5 minutes or until the sauce has reduced
and thickened and the chicken is cooked through.

Divide the chicken korma among bowls and serve with the
yoghurt drizzle.

Lean meat, fish, poultry, eggs, tofu: 1.5
Breads, cereals, legumes, starchy
  vegetables: 0
Dairy and dairy alternatives: 0
Low–moderate carb vegetables: 3
Healthy fats: 4

# TOFU AND MUSHROOM BURGER BOWLS

🍴 Serves 4    🕐 Preparation: 10 minutes
🍲 Cooking: 15 minutes    👨‍🍳 Difficulty: Low

8 field mushrooms, stems removed,
  seasoned with pepper
600 g firm tofu, cut into 4 steaks,
  seasoned with pepper
1 red onion, cut into thin wedges
1 x 200 g packet mixed leaf
  superleaf salad mix
⅓ cup (80 g) chilli and garlic pesto

Preheat a large chargrill pan over high heat. Add the mushrooms and cook for 4 minutes each side or until golden and just tender. Transfer to a plate.

Chargrill the tofu and onion for 2 minutes each side or until golden and the onion is just tender. Transfer to a plate.

Divide the salad mix among serving bowls. Add a mushroom to each bowl, cup side up, then top with a tofu steak, some onion and drizzle with a little pesto. Top with the remaining mushrooms, cup side down. Drizzle with the remaining pesto and serve.

**UNITS PER SERVE**

Lean meat, fish, poultry, eggs, tofu: **1.5**
Breads, cereals, legumes, starchy
   vegetables: **0**
Dairy and dairy alternatives: **0**
Low–moderate carb vegetables: **1**
Healthy fats: **2.5**

Serves 4    Preparation: 15 minutes
Cooking: 10 minutes    Difficulty: Low

600 g lean uncrumbed pork
   schnitzels, seasoned with pepper
2 tablespoons sesame seeds
¼ cup (60 ml) salt-reduced soy sauce
1 x 350 g kaleslaw kit
   (dressing sachet discarded)
2 tablespoons sliced pickled
   ginger, shredded
160 g avocado, chopped into wedges
1 x 5 g packet roasted seaweed nori
   snack, crumbled

Combine the pork, sesame seeds and 2 tablespoons soy sauce in a bowl and toss to coat.

Preheat a large non-stick frying pan over high heat. Add the pork and cook for 3 minutes each side or until golden and cooked to medium. Transfer to a plate.

Combine the slaw, ginger and remaining soy sauce and divide among serving bowls.

Thinly slice the pork, then arrange next to the slaw. Add the avocado and nori and serve warm.

Lean meat, fish, poultry, eggs, tofu: 1.5
Breads, cereals, legumes, starchy
   vegetables: 0
Dairy and dairy alternatives: 1
Low–moderate carb vegetables: 2
Healthy fats: 1

# BARBECUED SALSA VERDE LAMB

🍴 Serves 4   🕐 Preparation: 10 minutes
♨ Cooking: 5 minutes   👐 Difficulty: Low

600 g heart-smart lamb, diced
   and seasoned with pepper
200 g cherry tomatoes
80 g haloumi, chopped
1 x 500 g packet broccoli and
   cauliflower rice
100 g baby spinach leaves
1 x 35 g sachet fresh salsa verde
   finishing drizzle

Preheat the chargrill and flat plates on a barbecue to high. Add the lamb to the chargrill plate and the tomatoes and haloumi to the flat plate. Cook for 5 minutes, turning constantly, until everything is golden and the lamb is cooked to medium.

Meanwhile, heat a large, deep non-stick frying pan over high heat. Add the broccoli and cauliflower rice and cook for 2 minutes, tossing occasionally. Add the spinach and cook, tossing, for 1 minute or until just wilted.

Divide the spinach rice among plates and top with the lamb, tomatoes and haloumi. Drizzle with the salsa verde and serve.

Lean meat, fish, poultry, eggs, tofu: **1.5**

Breads, cereals, legumes, starchy
   vegetables: **0**

Dairy and dairy alternatives: **0.5**

Low–moderate carb vegetables: **1.5**

Healthy fats: **3**

# CHERMOULA CHICKEN AND VEGETABLES

7 G CARB PER SERVE

🍴 **Serves 4**    🕐 **Preparation: 15 minutes**
🍲 **Cooking: 15 minutes**    ⚙ **Difficulty: Low**

COOKS IN **UNDER 15 MINS**

1 tablespoon Moroccan seasoning

1 teaspoon fresh garlic paste

2 teaspoons fresh coriander herb paste

2 teaspoons fresh parsley herb paste

600 g lean chicken tenderloins,
   sliced diagonally

2 tablespoons olive oil

2 x 250 g packets zucchini spaghetti

2 bunches broccolini, trimmed

100 g green olives stuffed with feta
   (approximately 50 g olives and
   50 g feta)

flat-leaf parsley leaves and lime
   wedges, to serve

Combine the Moroccan seasoning, pastes, chicken and half the oil in a bowl. Season with freshly ground black pepper.

Heat the remaining oil in a large non-stick frying pan over high heat. Add the zucchini spaghetti, broccolini and ¼ cup (60 ml) water and cook, tossing carefully, for 2 minutes or until just tender. Remove the pan from the heat, add the olives and gently toss to combine. Divide the mixture among bowls and cover to keep warm.

Reheat the pan over high heat. Cook the chicken in three batches for 4 minutes each, tossing constantly, until cooked and nicely browned. Transfer each batch to a bowl before adding the next.

Spoon the chicken over the vegetable mixture in the bowls and top with the parsley leaves. Serve with the lime wedges.

# SIMPLE TUNA BAKE

**9 G CARB PER SERVE**

Lean meat, fish, poultry, eggs, tofu: **1.5**
Breads, cereals, legumes, starchy
  vegetables: **0**
Dairy and dairy alternatives: **1**
Low–moderate carb vegetables: **3**
Healthy fats: **2**

---

1 x 500 g packet frozen mixed
  winter vegetables
1 x 410 g tin rich and thick basil and
  garlic chopped tomatoes
600 g drained tinned tuna chunks
  in springwater (see note)
200 g reduced-fat natural yoghurt
60 g cheddar, finely grated
80 g slivered almonds
small basil leaves and lemon wedges,
  to serve

🍴 **Serves 4**   🕐 **Preparation: 15 minutes**
〰 **Cooking: 15 minutes**   🎩 **Difficulty: Low**

COOKS IN **UNDER 15 MINS**

Preheat the oven to 220°C (200°C fan-forced).

Combine the frozen vegetables, tomatoes and tuna in a 7 cm deep rectangular or oval baking dish and season with freshly ground black pepper.

Combine the yoghurt and cheddar, then spoon over the mixture in the dish. Sprinkle the almonds over the top and season with freshly ground black pepper. Bake for 15 minutes or until heated through and the top is golden.

Sprinkle the tuna bake with the basil leaves and serve with the lemon wedges.

**Note:** Because you will be draining off quite a bit of liquid, you will need two 425 g tins of tuna in springwater to have the required quantity for this recipe. Store the leftover tuna in an airtight container in the fridge for up to 3 days.

# VIETNAMESE GARLIC PEPPER PRAWNS

**4 G CARB PER SERVE**

**UNITS PER SERVE**

Lean meat, fish, poultry, eggs, tofu: **1.5**

Breads, cereals, legumes, starchy
  vegetables: **0**

Dairy and dairy alternatives: **0**

Low–moderate carb vegetables: **2**

Healthy fats: **2**

---

🍴 **Serves 4**   🕐 **Preparation: 15 minutes**
🍲 **Cooking: 5 minutes**   🎚 **Difficulty: Low**

---

1 tablespoon garlic pepper seasoning

600 g peeled and deveined raw prawns

1 tablespoon sunflower oil

1 x 250 g packet vegetable
  superfoods stir-fry mix

300 g bean sprouts

½ cup mint leaves

½ cup coriander leaves

**DRESSING**

1 teaspoon fish sauce

2 tablespoons lime juice

½ teaspoon fresh chilli herb paste

½ teaspoon fresh ginger herb paste

2 teaspoons sunflower oil

To make the dressing, whisk together all the ingredients in a jug. Season with freshly ground black pepper.

Combine the garlic pepper seasoning and prawns in a bowl. Heat the oil in a large non-stick wok over high heat, add the prawns and stir-fry for 3 minutes. Add the vegetable mix and stir-fry for 1 minute.

Remove the wok from the heat. Add the sprouts, mint, coriander and dressing and toss well to combine. Divide among plates or bowls and serve.

# PEPPER STEAK MUSHROOM MELT

**UNITS PER SERVE**

Lean meat, fish, poultry, eggs, tofu: **1.5**

Breads, cereals, legumes, starchy vegetables: **0**

Dairy and dairy alternatives: **1**

Low–moderate carb vegetables: **3.5**

Healthy fats: **2**

🍴 Serves 4   🕐 Preparation: 15 minutes
🍲 Cooking: 15 minutes   🎲 Difficulty: Low

600 g lean beef strips, seasoned with pepper

1 tablespoon pepper steak seasoning

2 tablespoons sunflower oil

8 field mushrooms, stems removed, seasoned with pepper

1 x 120 g packet baby spinach leaves

1 x 410 g tin rich and thick mixed herbs chopped tomatoes

100 g mozzarella, grated

1 x 270 g packet Greek-style salad kit (dressing sachet discarded)

lemon wedges, to serve

Combine the beef, pepper steak seasoning and oil in a bowl. Heat a large non-stick frying pan over high heat. Cook the beef in three batches for 4 minutes each, tossing constantly, until well browned and cooked to medium. Transfer each batch to a bowl before adding the next.

Meanwhile, preheat the oven grill to high. Place the mushrooms, cup side up, in a large baking dish so they sit side by side. Grill for 5 minutes. Remove and top with the spinach, then spoon over the tomatoes. Grill for a further 2 minutes.

Scatter the beef over the mushroom mixture and top with the mozzarella. Grill for 2–3 minutes or until the cheese is melted and golden. Take the dish to the table and serve with the salad and lemon wedges.

# THAI SALMON AND VEGGIE BRAISE

**UNITS PER SERVE**

Lean meat, fish, poultry, eggs, tofu: **1.5**

Breads, cereals, legumes, starchy vegetables: **0**

Dairy and dairy alternatives: **0**

Low–moderate carb vegetables: **1.5**

Healthy fats: **2.5**

🍴 **Serves 4**  🕐 **Preparation: 10 minutes**
〰 **Cooking: 15 minutes**  👩‍🍳 **Difficulty: Low**

---

2 cups (500 ml) salt-reduced vegetable stock

¼ cup (60 g) fresh Thai herb paste

1 x 500 g packet frozen Thai-style stir-fry vegetables

100 g baby spinach leaves

4 x 150 g skinless, boneless salmon fillets

80 g dry-roasted unsalted cashews, chopped

Combine the stock and herb paste in a large, deep non-stick frying pan over medium–high heat and bring to a rapid simmer. Cook for 5 minutes or until the stock has reduced by one-third.

Add the frozen vegetables and spinach and stir well to combine. Place the salmon on top. Bring back to a rapid simmer and cook uncovered and untouched for 6–8 minutes or until the salmon is cooked to your liking and the stock has reduced by another third. Sprinkle with the cashews and serve.

# CREAMY PESTO CHICKEN WITH VEGGIE MASH

UNITS PER SERVE

Lean meat, fish, poultry, eggs, tofu: 1.5

Breads, cereals, legumes, starchy vegetables: 0

Dairy and dairy alternatives: 1.5

Low–moderate carb vegetables: 2.5

Healthy fats: 4

🍴 Serves 4  🕐 Preparation: 15 minutes
♨ Cooking: 15 minutes  🍲 Difficulty: Low

200 g reduced-fat natural yoghurt

80 g parmesan, finely grated

¼ cup (60 g) fresh basil pesto

600 g lean chicken breast, diced and seasoned with pepper

500 g tomatoes

### VEGGIE MASH

150 g peeled, deseeded pumpkin, cut into 1 cm pieces

1 x 500 g packet frozen broccoli and cauliflower

⅔ cup (180 ml) salt-reduced chicken stock

Combine the yoghurt, parmesan and pesto in a large bowl. Season with freshly ground black pepper.

To make the veggie mash, place all the ingredients in a saucepan over medium heat. Cover and bring to a simmer, then remove the lid and cook, stirring occasionally, for 10–12 minutes or until the stock has reduced to about 1 tablespoon and the vegetables are very tender. Remove the pan from the heat and roughly mash. Season with freshly ground black pepper.

Meanwhile, heat a large chargrill pan over high heat. Cook the chicken in three batches for 4 minutes each, tossing constantly, until well browned and cooked through. Transfer each batch to the bowl with the yoghurt mixture and toss to coat before adding the next.

Chargrill the tomatoes, turning occasionally, for 3 minutes or until the skins start to blister.

Divide the veggie mash among plates. Top with the pesto chicken and tomatoes and serve.

Lean meat, fish, poultry, eggs, tofu: **1.5**
Breads, cereals, legumes, starchy
   vegetables: **0**
Dairy and dairy alternatives: **0**
Low–moderate carb vegetables: **1.5**
Healthy fats: **2**

# GARLIC CHICKEN AND CHINESE BROCCOLI

🍴 **Serves 4**   🕐 **Preparation: 15 minutes**
🍲 **Cooking: 10 minutes**   🍳 **Difficulty: Low**

2 tablespoons sunflower oil
5 cm piece ginger, cut into
   thin matchsticks
6 cloves garlic, thinly sliced
600 g lean chicken breast, diced
2 large bunches Chinese broccoli,
   trimmed and cut into 4 cm lengths
2 spring onions, thinly sliced

Heat the oil in a large non-stick wok over high heat, add the ginger, garlic and chicken and stir-fry for 5 minutes.

Add the broccoli and ¼ cup (60 ml) water to the wok and stir-fry for 2 minutes. Add the spring onion and stir-fry for 1 minute or until the chicken is cooked through. Divide among bowls and serve.

# THAI BEEF SALAD

**UNITS PER SERVE**

Lean meat, fish, poultry, eggs, tofu: **1.5**
Breads, cereals, legumes, starchy
  vegetables: **0**
Dairy and dairy alternatives: **0**
Low–moderate carb vegetables: **1.5**
Healthy fats: **0**

Serves 4   Preparation: 15 minutes
Cooking: 5 minutes   Difficulty: Low

600 g lean beef stir-fry strips
1 long red chilli, finely chopped
2 teaspoons fish sauce
3 teaspoons fresh coriander herb paste
1 cup small basil leaves
1 small red onion, very thinly sliced
1 x 300 g packet mixed baby
  leaf salad mix
1 cup bean sprouts
lime wedges, to serve

Heat a large non-stick wok over high heat, add the beef, chilli,
fish sauce and herb paste and stir-fry for 5 minutes or until the
beef is cooked.

Remove the wok from the heat, add the basil and onion and toss
together well.

Combine the salad mix and sprouts in a bowl. Divide among plates
and top with the beef mixture. Serve with the lime wedges.

Lean meat, fish, poultry, eggs, tofu: **1.5**

Breads, cereals, legumes, starchy
vegetables: **0**

Dairy and dairy alternatives: **0**

Low–moderate carb vegetables: **2**

Healthy fats: **2**

# JAPANESE-STYLE CHICKEN AND GREENS

7 G
CARB PER
SERVE

🍴 **Serves 4**    🕐 **Preparation: 15 minutes**
〰 **Cooking: 10 minutes**    ⑨ **Difficulty: Low**

1 tablespoon sunflower oil

600 g lean chicken breast strips

2 tablespoons salt-reduced soy sauce

2 teaspoons fresh garlic paste

1 tablespoon white wine vinegar

2 bunches broccolini, trimmed and
halved lengthways

400 g snowpeas, trimmed and
halved diagonally

2 teaspoons sesame seeds, toasted

Heat the oil in a large non-stick wok over high heat, add the
chicken, soy sauce and garlic paste and stir-fry for 5 minutes.

Add the vinegar, broccolini and ¼ cup (60 ml) water to the wok
and stir-fry for 2 minutes. Add the snowpeas and sesame seeds and
stir-fry for 1 minute or until the chicken is cooked through. Divide
among bowls and serve.

# GARLIC SESAME PRAWNS

**UNITS PER SERVE**

Lean meat, fish, poultry, eggs, tofu: **1.5**
Breads, cereals, legumes, starchy
   vegetables: **0**
Dairy and dairy alternatives: **0**
Low–moderate carb vegetables: **1**
Healthy fats: **2.5**

Serves 4    Preparation: 15 minutes
Cooking: 5 minutes    Difficulty: Low

2 tablespoons sunflower oil
600 g peeled and deveined raw
   small prawns
2 teaspoons crushed garlic
2 tablespoons sesame seeds
1 large red capsicum, seeded and
   cut into thin strips
2 bunches thin asparagus, trimmed
   and cut diagonally into 4 cm lengths
4 spring onions, cut into 4 cm lengths
1 tablespoon salt-reduced soy sauce

Heat the oil in a large non-stick wok over high heat, add the
prawns, garlic and sesame seeds and stir-fry for 30 seconds.

Add the capsicum, asparagus, spring onion and soy sauce to
the wok and stir-fry for 3 minutes. Divide among bowls and serve.

**UNITS PER SERVE**

Lean meat, fish, poultry, eggs, tofu: **1.5**

Breads, cereals, legumes, starchy
vegetables: **0**

Dairy and dairy alternatives: **0**

Low–moderate carb vegetables: **1.5**

Healthy fats: **3**

1 tablespoon sunflower oil

2 tablespoons green curry paste

600 g firm tofu, sliced

2 large sticks celery,
thinly sliced diagonally

2 bunches asparagus, trimmed and
cut diagonally into 2 cm pieces

300 g sugar snap peas, trimmed

⅓ cup (80 ml) salt-reduced
vegetable stock

½ cup basil leaves

# GREEN CURRIED TOFU AND GREENS

🍴 **Serves 4**   🕐 **Preparation: 15 minutes**
♨ **Cooking: 5 minutes**   🖐 **Difficulty: Low**

COOKS IN **UNDER 5 MINS**

Heat the oil in a large non-stick wok over high heat, add the curry paste, tofu and celery and stir-fry for 3 minutes.

Add the asparagus, sugar snaps and stock to the wok and stir-fry for 1 minute. Remove the wok from the heat, add the basil and toss to combine. Divide among plates or bowls and serve.

# KOREAN-STYLE CHICKEN WITH CUCUMBER

**UNITS PER SERVE**

Lean meat, fish, poultry, eggs, tofu: **1.5**
Breads, cereals, legumes, starchy
    vegetables: **0**
Dairy and dairy alternatives: **0**
Low–moderate carb vegetables: **2.5**
Healthy fats: **0**

🍴 **Serves 4**  🕐 **Preparation: 15 minutes**
🍲 **Cooking: 10 minutes**  👨‍🍳 **Difficulty: Low**

**COOKS IN UNDER 10 MINS**

600 g lean chicken breast strips
¼ cup (60 ml) honey soy marinade
    and stir-fry sauce
1 tablespoon hot chilli sauce
2 x 300 g packets superfood
    stir-fry vegetables
2 spring onions, thinly sliced
4 Lebanese cucumbers,
    thinly sliced diagonally

Heat a large non-stick wok over high heat, add the chicken, honey soy sauce and hot chilli sauce and stir-fry for 5 minutes or until the chicken is cooked.

Add the stir-fry vegetables and spring onion to the wok and stir-fry for 3 minutes. Divide among plates or bowls and serve with the cucumber.

**UNITS PER SERVE**

Lean meat, fish, poultry, eggs, tofu: **1.5**

Breads, cereals, legumes, starchy
  vegetables: **0**

Dairy and dairy alternatives: **0**

Low–moderate carb vegetables: **1.5**

Healthy fats: **2**

# GINGER AND LIME PORK

🍴 **Serves 4**   🕐 **Preparation: 15 minutes**
🍲 **Cooking: 10 minutes**   🏅 **Difficulty: Low**

2 tablespoons sunflower oil

600 g lean pork stir-fry strips

4 kaffir lime leaves,
  very finely shredded

5 cm piece ginger, cut into
  thin matchsticks

300 g red cabbage, shredded

½ cup (125 ml) salt-reduced
  chicken stock

1 x 450 g packet frozen steam fresh
  beans, broccoli and sugar snap peas

finely grated zest and juice of 2 limes

Heat the oil in a large non-stick wok over high heat, add the pork, kaffir lime leaves and ginger and stir-fry for 5 minutes. Add the cabbage and stock and stir-fry for 3 minutes.

Add the vegetables to the wok and stir-fry for 2 minutes. Remove the wok from the heat and toss through the lime zest and juice. Divide among plates or bowls and serve.

# CHILLI SOY FLATHEAD

**UNITS PER SERVE**

Lean meat, fish, poultry, eggs, tofu: **1.5**

Breads, cereals, legumes, starchy
  vegetables: **0**

Dairy and dairy alternatives: **0**

Low–moderate carb vegetables: **2**

Healthy fats: **2**

🍴 **Serves 4**     🕐 **Preparation: 15 minutes**
〰 **Cooking: 10 minutes**     👨‍🍳 **Difficulty: Low**

2 tablespoons sunflower oil

1 bunch choy sum, cut into 4 cm lengths

½ cup coriander leaves

2 teaspoons fresh garlic paste

2 long red chillies, seeded and
  thinly sliced

1 spring onion, cut into 5 cm lengths

1 green capsicum, seeded and cut
  into 2 cm pieces

600 g skinless, boneless flathead fillets,
  cut into 4 cm pieces

2 tablespoons salt-reduced soy sauce

Heat 1 tablespoon oil in a large non-stick wok over high heat, add the choy sum and coriander and stir-fry for 2 minutes or until just wilted. Transfer to serving plates.

Heat the remaining oil in the wok over high heat, add the garlic paste, chilli, spring onion and capsicum and stir-fry for 2 minutes.

Add the fish and soy sauce to the wok and stir-fry for 2 minutes or until the fish is just cooked. Spoon over the choy sum mixture and serve.

Lean meat, fish, poultry, eggs, tofu: **1.5**
Breads, cereals, legumes, starchy
 vegetables: **0**
Dairy and dairy alternatives: **0**
Low–moderate carb vegetables: **2.5**
Healthy fats: **3**

# STICKY PORK AND CRISPY SALAD

**10 G CARB PER SERVE**

🍴 **Serves 4**   🕐 **Preparation: 15 minutes**
🍲 **Cooking: 10 minutes**   👨‍🍳 **Difficulty: Low**

1 tablespoon sunflower oil
600 g lean pork stir-fry strips,
 seasoned with pepper
3 teaspoons fresh garlic paste
2 tablespoons hoisin sauce
juice of 2 lemons

**CRISPY SALAD**
400 g green cabbage,
 very finely shredded
1 cup small mint leaves
1 cup bean sprouts
2 spring onions, thinly sliced diagonally
300 g broccoli florets, chopped
80 g slivered almonds,
 toasted and chopped

To make the crispy salad, combine all the ingredients in a bowl. Divide among serving plates.

Heat the oil in a large non-stick wok over high heat, add the pork and garlic paste and stir-fry for 5 minutes. Add the hoisin sauce and lemon juice and stir-fry for 1 minute or until well combined and the pork is cooked through.

Spoon the hot pork mixture alongside the crispy salad and serve.

Lean meat, fish, poultry, eggs, tofu: **1.5**

Breads, cereals, legumes, starchy
  vegetables: **0**

Dairy and dairy alternatives: **0**

Low–moderate carb vegetables: **2**

Healthy fats: **2**

# BEEF AND PUMPKIN MASSAMAN

🍽 **Serves 4**   🕐 **Preparation: 15 minutes**
🍲 **Cooking: 10 minutes**   🍴 **Difficulty: Low**

2 tablespoons massaman curry paste

600 g lean beef stir-fry strips

1 small red onion, chopped

150 g peeled, seeded pumpkin,
  cut into matchsticks

2 bunches choy sum, stems sliced,
  leaves torn

½ cup (125 ml) salt-reduced
  chicken stock

Heat a large non-stick wok over high heat, add the curry paste,
beef and onion and stir-fry for 5 minutes or until the beef is cooked.

Add the pumpkin, choy sum and stock to the wok and stir-fry for
3 minutes. Divide among plates or bowls and serve.

Lean meat, fish, poultry, eggs, tofu: **1.5**
Breads, cereals, legumes, starchy
  vegetables: **0**
Dairy and dairy alternatives: **0**
Low–moderate carb vegetables: **1**
Healthy fats: **4**

1 tablespoon sunflower oil
600 g lean beef strips
1 tablespoon hoisin sauce
2 tablespoons salt-reduced soy sauce
2 x 300 g packets supergreen
  stir-fry vegetables
120 g blanched almonds, toasted
  and chopped

# BEEF AND ALMONDS

🍴 Serves 4   🕐 Preparation: 15 minutes
〰 Cooking: 10 minutes   👨‍🍳 Difficulty: Low

**COOKS IN UNDER 10 MINS**

Heat the oil in a large non-stick wok over high heat, add the beef and hoisin sauce and stir-fry for 5 minutes or until the beef is cooked.

Add the soy sauce and vegetables to the wok and stir-fry for 3 minutes. Remove the wok from the heat, add the almonds and toss to combine. Divide among plates or bowls and serve.

## UNITS PER SERVE

Lean meat, fish, poultry, eggs, tofu: **1.5**

Breads, cereals, legumes, starchy
 vegetables: **0**

Dairy and dairy alternatives: **0**

Low–moderate carb vegetables: **1.5**

Healthy fats: **0**

600 g lean lamb backstrap,
 very thinly sliced

2 tablespoons hoisin sauce

1 tablespoon salt-reduced soy sauce

2 teaspoons fresh garlic paste

2 large sticks celery,
 thinly sliced diagonally

4 spring onions, thinly sliced diagonally

2 x 250 g packets fresh
 zucchini spaghetti

# HOISIN LAMB, CELERY AND ZOODLES

🍴 Serves 4    🕐 Preparation: 15 minutes

〰 Cooking: 10 minutes    👨‍🍳 Difficulty: Low

**COOKS IN UNDER 10 MINS**

Heat a large non-stick wok over high heat, add the lamb, hoisin sauce, soy sauce and garlic paste and stir-fry for 5 minutes. Add the celery and spring onion and stir-fry for 2 minutes.

Toss the zucchini spaghetti and ¼ cup (60 ml) water into the wok and stir-fry for 1 minute. Divide among plates or bowls and serve.

# FISH CURRY WITH CORIANDER DRESSING

6 G CARB PER SERVE

**UNITS PER SERVE**

Lean meat, fish, poultry, eggs, tofu: **1.5**
Breads, cereals, legumes, starchy
   vegetables: **0**
Dairy and dairy alternatives: **0**
Low–moderate carb vegetables: **1.5**
Healthy fats: **2**

🍴 **Serves 4**   🕐 **Preparation: 15 minutes**
〰 **Cooking: 10 minutes**   👨‍🍳 **Difficulty: Low**

2 tablespoons yellow curry paste
1 small red onion, cut into thin wedges
200 g baby green beans, trimmed
400 g broccoli florets
½ cup (125 ml) salt-reduced
   chicken stock
600 g skinless, boneless ling fillet,
   cut into 3 cm pieces

**CORIANDER DRESSING**

¼ teaspoon sesame oil
1 cup coriander leaves
finely grated zest and juice
   of 2 lemons

To make the coriander dressing, combine all the ingredients in a jug. Season with freshly ground black pepper.

Heat a large non-stick wok over high heat, add the curry paste, onion, beans, broccoli and half the stock and stir-fry for 3 minutes.

Add the ling and the remaining stock to the wok and stir-fry for 3 minutes or until the ling is just cooked. Divide among plates or bowls, drizzle with the coriander dressing and serve.

# SINGAPORE-STYLE TOFU ZOODLES

**UNITS PER SERVE**

Lean meat, fish, poultry, eggs, tofu: **1.5**
Breads, cereals, legumes, starchy
   vegetables: **0**
Dairy and dairy alternatives: **0**
Low–moderate carb vegetables: **3**
Healthy fats: **2**

Serves 4   Preparation: 15 minutes
Cooking: 5 minutes   Difficulty: Low

2 tablespoons sunflower oil
2 spring onions, chopped diagonally
1 red capsicum, seeded and chopped
600 g firm tofu, chopped
1 tablespoon curry powder
1 tablespoon hoisin sauce
2 tablespoons salt-reduced soy sauce
100 g baby spinach leaves
1½ cups bean sprouts
2 x 250 g packets fresh
   zucchini spaghetti

Heat the oil in a large non-stick wok over high heat, add the spring onion, capsicum, tofu and curry powder and stir-fry for 3 minutes.

Add the hoisin sauce, soy sauce and spinach to the wok and stir-fry for 1 minute. Remove the wok from the heat, add the sprouts and zucchini spaghetti and toss to combine. Divide among plates or bowls and serve.

Lean meat, fish, poultry, eggs, tofu: **1.5**

Breads, cereals, legumes, starchy
vegetables: **0**

Dairy and dairy alternatives: **0**

Low–moderate carb vegetables: **2**

Healthy fats: **2**

# FIVE-SPICE PORK AND MUSHROOMS

🍴 **Serves 4**   🕐 **Preparation: 15 minutes**

🍳 **Cooking: 10 minutes**   🍲 **Difficulty: Low**

2 tablespoons sunflower oil

600 g lean pork fillet, thinly sliced

1 tablespoon Chinese five-spice powder

3 x 150 g packets exotic stir-fry
mushroom mix, sliced

½ cup (125 ml) salt-reduced
chicken stock

2 bunches (6 pieces) baby bok choy,
halved lengthways

Heat the oil in a large non-stick wok over high heat, add the pork and five-spice powder and stir-fry for 5 minutes. Add the mushroom mix and half the stock and stir-fry for 2 minutes.

Add the bok choy and remaining stock to the wok and stir-fry for 2 minutes. Divide among plates or bowls and serve.

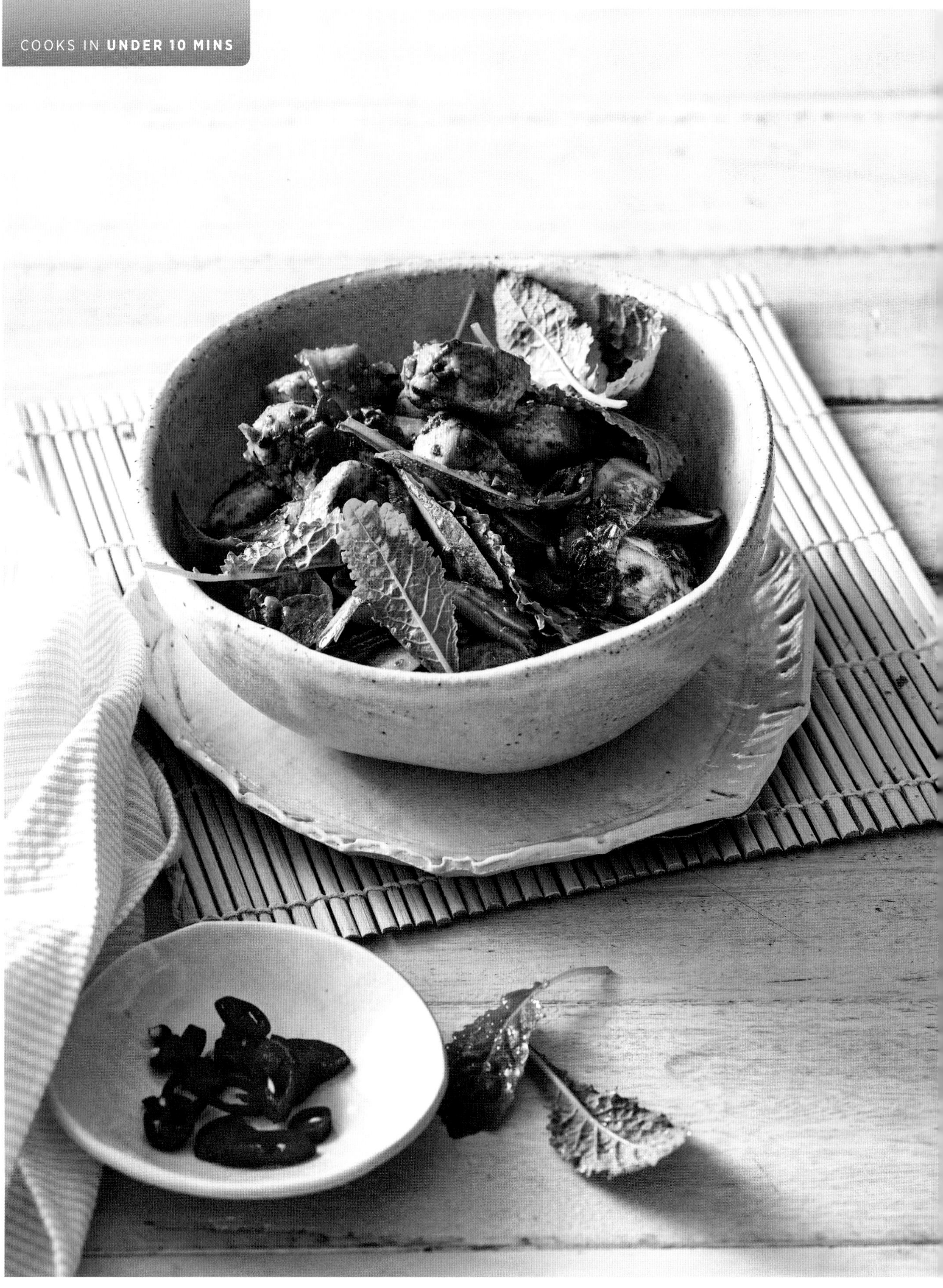

Lean meat, fish, poultry, eggs, tofu: **1.5**
Breads, cereals, legumes, starchy
    vegetables: **0**
Dairy and dairy alternatives: **0**
Low–moderate carb vegetables: **1**
Healthy fats: **3**

# LEMONGRASS CHILLI CHICKEN AND KALE

🍴 **Serves 4**   🕐 **Preparation: 15 minutes**
♨ **Cooking: 10 minutes**   🍳 **Difficulty: Low**

2 tablespoons sunflower oil
1 tablespoon fresh lemongrass
    herb paste
2 long red chillies, thinly
    sliced diagonally
600 g lean chicken tenderloins,
    chopped and seasoned with pepper
2 zucchini, halved lengthways and
    thinly sliced
handful baby kale leaves or 8 large kale
    leaves, white stems removed, torn

Heat the oil in a large non-stick wok over high heat, add the herb paste, chilli and chicken and stir-fry for 5 minutes until the chicken is cooked.

Add the zucchini, kale and ¼ cup (60 ml) water to the wok and stir-fry for 1 minute or until the kale has just wilted. Divide among plates or bowls and serve.

Lean meat, fish, poultry, eggs, tofu: **1.5**
Breads, cereals, legumes, starchy
   vegetables: **0**
Dairy and dairy alternatives: **1**
Low–moderate carb vegetables: **2**
Healthy fats: **0.5**

# GREEK LAMB AND BEAN SALAD

10 G CARB PER SERVE

ONLY **6** INGREDIENTS

🍴 **Serves 4**  🕐 **Preparation: 15 minutes**
♨ **Cooking: 10 minutes**  🎩 **Difficulty: Low**

1 tablespoon no-added-salt garlic
   and herb seasoning
600 g extra-trim Frenched lamb cutlets
400 g baby green beans, trimmed
2 x 270 g packets Greek-style salad kit
   (dressing sachet discarded)
⅓ cup (80 ml) fat-free caesar dressing
80 g reduced-fat Greek feta, crumbled

Preheat a barbecue chargrill plate to high.

Sprinkle the garlic and herb seasoning over the lamb, coating well on all sides. Chargrill the lamb and beans for 6 minutes, turning occasionally, until the lamb is golden and cooked to medium. Transfer to serving plates.

Meanwhile, combine the salad kit, dressing and feta in a bowl and season with freshly ground black pepper.

Serve the lamb cutlets and beans with the salad.

# BEEF STEAK AND PANANG VEGETABLES

**UNITS PER SERVE**

Lean meat, fish, poultry, eggs, tofu: **1.5**
Breads, cereals, legumes, starchy
  vegetables: **0**
Dairy and dairy alternatives: **0**
Low–moderate carb vegetables: **2**
Healthy fats: **3**

🍴 **Serves 4**   🕐 **Preparation: 20 minutes**
🍲 **Cooking: 15 minutes**   🍳 **Difficulty: Low**

ONLY
**6**
INGREDIENTS

1 tablespoon sunflower oil
4 x 150 g lean beef fillet steaks,
  seasoned with pepper
2 tablespoons panang curry paste
1 x 500 g packet frozen Thai-style
  stir-fry vegetables
1 bunch bok choy, leaves separated
lime wedges, to serve

Heat the oil in a large, deep non-stick frying pan over high heat.
Add the steaks and cook for 3 minutes each side for medium.
Transfer to a board.

Add the curry paste and vegetables to the pan and cook, tossing,
for 3 minutes. Add the bok choy and ⅓ cup (80 ml) water and
simmer for 2 minutes or until the sauce has reduced and thickened.

Divide the panang vegetables among shallow bowls. Slice the steak
diagonally, then arrange on top. Serve with the lime wedges.

Lean meat, fish, poultry, eggs, tofu: **1.5**
Breads, cereals, legumes, starchy
   vegetables: **0**
Dairy and dairy alternatives: **1**
Low–moderate carb vegetables: **2**
Healthy fats: **3**

# ALMOND-CRUSTED CHICKEN AND BROCCOLI BAKE

**6 G CARB PER SERVE**

🍽 **Serves 4**  🕐 **Preparation: 20 minutes**
♨ **Cooking: 15 minutes**  🖐 **Difficulty: Low**

1 red onion, chopped
2 zucchini, cut into 1 cm pieces
300 g small broccoli florets
600 g lean chicken breast strips,
   seasoned with pepper
1 teaspoon dried mixed herbs
1 tablespoon olive oil
lemon wedges, to serve

**ALMOND CRUST**
80 g almond meal
2 tablespoons finely chopped chives
finely grated zest and juice
   of 1 large lemon
80 g cheddar, finely grated

Preheat the oven to 220°C (200°C fan-forced). Line a large shallow baking dish with baking paper.

To make the almond crust, combine all the ingredients in a bowl and season with freshly ground black pepper.

Mix together the onion, zucchini, broccoli, chicken, dried herbs and oil and season with freshly ground black pepper. Spread evenly over the prepared tray and sprinkle with the almond crust. Roast for 15 minutes or until golden and the chicken is cooked through.

Divide the chicken mixture among plates and serve with the lemon wedges.

# PRAWN RED CURRY AND GREENS

**UNITS PER SERVE**

Lean meat, fish, poultry, eggs, tofu: **1.5**
Breads, cereals, legumes, starchy
  vegetables: **0**
Dairy and dairy alternatives: **0**
Low–moderate carb vegetables: **2**
Healthy fats: **2**

Serves 4    Preparation: 15 minutes
Cooking: 10 minutes    Difficulty: Low

2 tablespoons red curry paste
600 g peeled and deveined small
  raw prawns
2 zucchini, chopped
1 small green capsicum,
  seeded and chopped
1 bunch Chinese broccoli, trimmed
  and cut into 4 cm lengths
½ cup (125 ml) salt-reduced
  chicken stock
small coriander sprigs and lime
  wedges, to serve

Heat a large, deep non-stick frying pan over high heat. Add the curry paste and prawns and cook, tossing, for 30 seconds.

Add the zucchini and capsicum and cook, tossing, for 2 minutes. Add the broccoli and stock and simmer for 3 minutes or until the sauce has reduced by half.

Divide among bowls and sprinkle with the coriander sprigs. Serve with the lime wedges.

Lean meat, fish, poultry, eggs, tofu: **1.5**

Breads, cereals, legumes, starchy
vegetables: **0**

Dairy and dairy alternatives: **0.5**

Low–moderate carb vegetables: **2**

Healthy fats: **2**

# GRILLED CHICKEN TIKKA WITH CUCUMBER YOGHURT SALAD

**10 G CARB PER SERVE**

🍴 **Serves 4**   🕐 **Preparation: 20 minutes**
🍲 **Cooking: 15 minutes**   🍳 **Difficulty: Low**

COOKS IN **UNDER 15 MINS**

600 g lean chicken tenderloins,
   halved lengthways

2 tablespoons tikka masala curry paste

2 bunches thin asparagus, trimmed

500 g cherry tomatoes

small coriander leaves and lemon
   wedges, to serve

### CUCUMBER YOGHURT SALAD

200 g reduced-fat natural yoghurt

finely grated zest and juice of
   1 large lemon

2 tablespoons chopped mint

2 Lebanese cucumbers,
   very thinly sliced into rounds

50 g baby rocket leaves

Preheat the oven grill to high. Combine the chicken, curry paste, asparagus and tomatoes in a bowl, then spread evenly over a large non-stick baking tray. Cook under the grill, turning everything once, for 12–15 minutes or until the chicken is golden and cooked through.

Meanwhile, to make the cucumber yoghurt salad, whisk together the yoghurt, lemon zest, lemon juice and mint in a large bowl. Add the cucumber and rocket and gently toss to combine. Season with freshly ground black pepper.

Divide the salad, chicken and vegetables among plates, sprinkle over some coriander leaves and serve with the lemon wedges.

# ROAST MUSTARD CHICKEN AND BRUSSELS SPROUTS WITH RADISH SALAD

**UNITS PER SERVE**

Lean meat, fish, poultry, eggs, tofu: **1.5**

Breads, cereals, legumes, starchy
vegetables: **0**

Dairy and dairy alternatives: **1**

Low–moderate carb vegetables: **2**

Healthy fats: **2.5**

🍴 **Serves 4**  🕐 **Preparation: 25 minutes**
🍲 **Cooking: 15 minutes**  🍳 **Difficulty: Low**

COOKS IN **UNDER 15 MINS**

2 tablespoons extra virgin olive oil

¼ cup (60 ml) red wine vinegar

2 tablespoons wholegrain mustard

600 g lean chicken breast, diced and
seasoned with pepper

300 g baby brussels sprouts, trimmed
and halved

**RADISH SALAD**

1 bunch baby radishes, very thinly
sliced into rounds

2 Lebanese cucumbers, peeled into
long thin ribbons

100 g baby bocconcini, torn

1 bunch flat-leaf parsley, leaves picked,
stems finely chopped

⅓ cup (80 ml) fat-free Italian dressing

Preheat the oven to 220°C (200°C fan-forced). Line a large baking tray with baking paper.

Combine all the ingredients in a bowl and season with freshly ground black pepper. Spread evenly over the prepared tray and roast for 15 minutes or until the chicken is cooked through.

Meanwhile, to make the radish salad, place all the ingredients in a bowl and toss together.

Divide the chicken mixture among plates and serve with the radish salad.

# BAKED TOFU RATATOUILLE

**UNITS PER SERVE**

Lean meat, fish, poultry, eggs, tofu: **1.5**

Breads, cereals, legumes, starchy vegetables: **0**

Dairy and dairy alternatives: **0**

Low–moderate carb vegetables: **4**

Healthy fats: **2**

**Serves 4**  **Preparation: 20 minutes**
**Cooking: 15 minutes**  **Difficulty: Low**

1 eggplant, chopped
1 red capsicum, seeded and thinly sliced
1 red onion, thinly sliced
2 x 200 g punnets tomato medley mix
1 x 400 g tin cherry tomatoes
¼ cup thyme leaves
2 teaspoons fresh garlic paste
1 small bunch basil, leaves picked
60 g baby spinach leaves
600 g firm tofu, cut into 2 cm pieces
2 tablespoons olive oil

Preheat the oven to 220°C (200°C fan-forced).

Combine the eggplant, capsicum, onion, fresh and tinned tomatoes, thyme, garlic paste, basil and spinach in a large baking dish and scatter the tofu over the top. Drizzle with the oil and season with freshly ground black pepper.

Roast for 15 minutes or until golden and cooked.

# LAMB PAPRIKASH WITH SOURED ZOODLES

🍴 Serves 4    🕐 Preparation: 25 minutes
🍲 Cooking: 20 minutes    🎩 Difficulty: Low

**UNITS PER SERVE**

Lean meat, fish, poultry, eggs, tofu: **1.5**
Breads, cereals, legumes, starchy
   vegetables: **0**
Dairy and dairy alternatives: **0.5**
Low–moderate carb vegetables: **3.5**
Healthy fats: **2**

2 tablespoons olive oil
600 g lean lamb backstrap,
   seasoned with pepper
½ red onion, finely chopped
2 tablespoons sweet paprika
2 teaspoons fresh garlic paste
1 large red capsicum, seeded and
   thinly sliced
1 tablespoon salt-reduced tomato paste
1 x 400 g tin chopped tomatoes
2 cups (500 ml) salt-reduced beef stock
2 tablespoons red wine vinegar
1 bunch English spinach, leaves torn
flat-leaf parsley leaves, to serve

**SOURED ZOODLES**
200 g reduced-fat natural yoghurt
finely grated zest and juice of
   1 small lemon
½ red onion, finely chopped
2 x 250 g packets fresh
   zucchini spaghetti

Heat 1 tablespoon oil in a large, deep non-stick frying pan over high heat. Add the lamb and cook for 3 minutes each side for medium. Transfer to a board.

Heat the remaining oil in the pan. Add the onion, paprika, garlic paste and capsicum and cook, stirring, for 2 minutes. Add the tomato paste, tomatoes and stock. Bring to the boil and cook, stirring occasionally, for 10 minutes or until the sauce has reduced by half. Add the spinach and stir until just wilted. Season with freshly ground black pepper.

Meanwhile, to make the soured zoodles, whisk together the yoghurt, lemon zest and lemon juice in a bowl. Add the onion and zucchini and toss to combine. Season with freshly ground black pepper.

Divide the tomato mixture among plates. Slice the lamb, then arrange on top. Sprinkle with the parsley leaves and serve with the soured zoodles.

Lean meat, fish, poultry, eggs, tofu: **1.5**

Breads, cereals, legumes, starchy
vegetables: **0**

Dairy and dairy alternatives: **0**

Low–moderate carb vegetables: **3**

Healthy fats: **3**

# PUMPKIN AND TOFU TAGINE

🍴 **Serves 4**   🕐 **Preparation: 15 minutes**
🍲 **Cooking: 15 minutes**   👌 **Difficulty: Low**

2 tablespoons olive oil

1 tablespoon harissa seasoning

300 g peeled, seeded pumpkin,
cut into thin wedges

600 g firm tofu, cut into 2 cm pieces

2 zucchini, cut lengthways into quarters

1 x 500 g packet frozen broccoli and
cauliflower rice

Heat 1 tablespoon oil in a large, deep non-stick frying pan over high heat. Add the harissa, pumpkin, tofu and zucchini and cook, tossing, for 2 minutes. Add ½ cup (125 ml) water. Reduce the heat to medium and simmer, partially covered and stirring occasionally, for 10 minutes or until the vegetables are just tender.

Meanwhile, heat the remaining oil in a large non-stick wok over high heat. Add the broccoli and cauliflower rice and stir-fry for 2 minutes or until heated through and starting to crisp up.

Divide the rice and tofu tagine evenly among shallow bowls and serve.

# VIETNAMESE BEEF FRIED CAULIFLOWER RICE

**UNITS PER SERVE**

Lean meat, fish, poultry, eggs, tofu: **1.5**

Breads, cereals, legumes, starchy
 vegetables: **0**

Dairy and dairy alternatives: **0**

Low–moderate carb vegetables: **2.5**

Healthy fats: **1**

🍴 Serves 4    🕐 Preparation: 15 minutes

🍲 Cooking: 10 minutes    🖐 Difficulty: Low

1 tablespoon sunflower oil

600 g lean beef stir-fry strips

1 tablespoon ground white pepper

2 teaspoons fish sauce

1 long red chilli, finely chopped

2 teaspoons fresh ginger paste

1 bunch broccolini, trimmed
 and sliced diagonally

1 x 500 g packet frozen cauliflower rice

1 cup bean sprouts

small mint and coriander sprigs and
 lime wedges, to serve

Heat the oil in a large non-stick wok over high heat. Add the beef, pepper, fish sauce, chilli and ginger paste and stir-fry for 5 minutes or until the beef is cooked.

Add the broccolini, cauliflower rice and ¼ cup (60 ml) water to the wok and stir-fry for 3 minutes. Remove the wok from the heat, add the sprouts and toss to combine. Sprinkle with the mint and coriander sprigs and serve with the lime wedges.

# PORK WITH MUSHROOM STROGANOFF

**UNITS PER SERVE**

Lean meat, fish, poultry, eggs, tofu: **1.5**
Breads, cereals, legumes, starchy
   vegetables: **0**
Dairy and dairy alternatives: **0.5**
Low–moderate carb vegetables: **2.5**
Healthy fats: **2**

🍽 **Serves 4**　🕐 **Preparation: 15 minutes**
♨ **Cooking: 20 minutes**　🎩 **Difficulty: Low**

COOKS IN **UNDER 20 MINS**

2 tablespoons olive oil
4 x 150 g lean pork medallion steaks,
   seasoned with pepper
1 onion, finely chopped
2 teaspoons fresh garlic paste
600 g mixed mushrooms (button, Swiss
   brown, portobello), thickly sliced
2 beef stock cubes, crumbled
120 g baby spinach leaves
200 g reduced-fat natural yoghurt
2 tablespoons thyme leaves

Heat 1 tablespoon oil in a large, deep non-stick frying pan over high heat. Add the steaks and cook for 4 minutes each side or until cooked to your liking. Transfer to a plate.

Heat the remaining oil in the pan. Add the onion, garlic paste and mushroom and cook, tossing, for 5 minutes. Add the stock cubes, spinach and ¼ cup (60 ml) water and simmer for 3 minutes or until the spinach has wilted and the liquid has reduced and thickened.

Remove the pan from the heat and stand for 2 minutes, then gently stir in the yoghurt.

Divide the mushroom stroganoff among plates and top with the steak. Season with freshly ground black pepper, sprinkle with the thyme leaves and serve.

Lean meat, fish, poultry, eggs, tofu: **1.5**
Breads, cereals, legumes, starchy
  vegetables: **0**
Dairy and dairy alternatives: **0**
Low–moderate carb vegetables: **1.5**
Healthy fats: **0**

# LEMON AND HERB CHICKEN BAKE

6 G CARB PER SERVE

ONLY **6** INGREDIENTS

🍴 **Serves 4**    🕐 **Preparation: 20 minutes**
〰 **Cooking: 20 minutes**    👨‍🍳 **Difficulty: Low**

COOKS IN **UNDER 20 MINS**

1 x 500 g packet frozen broccoli
  and cauliflower rice
600 g lean chicken breast, diced
  and seasoned with pepper
2 tablespoons fresh garlic and onion
  with Italian herbs paste
1 lemon, cut into thin wedges
1 small red onion, thinly sliced
2 zucchini, thinly sliced into rounds

Preheat the oven to 220°C (200°C fan-forced). Line a large baking tray with baking paper.

Spread the frozen broccoli and cauliflower rice over the prepared tray.

Combine the chicken, paste, lemon, onion and zucchini in a bowl, then spoon it over the rice on the tray. Roast for 20 minutes or until the chicken is cooked through. Take the tray to the table and serve.

# GARLIC AND MINT CHICKEN WITH TOMATOES

**UNITS PER SERVE**

Lean meat, fish, poultry, eggs, tofu: **1.5**

Breads, cereals, legumes, starchy
  vegetables: **0**

Dairy and dairy alternatives: **0.5**

Low–moderate carb vegetables: **2.5**

Healthy fats: **1**

🍴 **Serves 4**   🕐 **Preparation: 25 minutes**
🍲 **Cooking: 15 minutes**   🍳 **Difficulty: Low**

600 g lean chicken tenderloins,
  seasoned with pepper

1 tablespoon olive oil

2 cloves garlic, thinly sliced

2 tablespoons thyme leaves

¼ cup chopped mint

500 g tomatoes

500 g baby yellow squash,
  halved horizontally

120 g baby spinach leaves

**DRESSING**

200 g reduced-fat natural yoghurt

½ teaspoon sweet paprika

⅓ cup (80 ml) fat-free balsamic
  Italian dressing

Preheat a barbecue chargrill plate to high.

Combine the chicken, oil, garlic, thyme and mint in a bowl and season with freshly ground black pepper. Chargrill the chicken, tomatoes and squash, turning occasionally, for 10–12 minutes or until golden and the chicken is cooked through. Transfer to a large bowl and immediately add the spinach. Gently toss to combine and slightly wilt the leaves.

Meanwhile, to make the dressing, mix together all the ingredients in a bowl. Season with freshly ground black pepper.

Divide the chicken mixture among plates, drizzle over the dressing and serve.

Lean meat, fish, poultry, eggs, tofu: **1.5**

Breads, cereals, legumes, starchy vegetables: **0**

Dairy and dairy alternatives: **0**

Low–moderate carb vegetables: **2**

Healthy fats: **2**

# TEX-MEX BAKED SALMON

🍴 **Serves 4**   🕐 **Preparation: 15 minutes**
♨ **Cooking: 10 minutes**   👩‍🍳 **Difficulty: Low**

2 x 300 g jars chunky tomato salsa

3 teaspoons smoked paprika

finely grated zest and juice of 1 lemon

4 x 150 g skinless, boneless salmon fillets

160 g avocado, sliced

small coriander sprigs, to serve

Preheat the oven to 220°C (200°C fan-forced).

Combine the salsa, paprika, lemon zest and juice in a shallow baking dish. Place the salmon on top and season with freshly ground black pepper. Roast for 15 minutes or until the salmon is cooked.

Scatter the avocado and coriander over the top and serve.

Lean meat, fish, poultry, eggs, tofu: **1.5**
Breads, cereals, legumes, starchy
  vegetables: **0**
Dairy and dairy alternatives: **0**
Low–moderate carb vegetables: **2**
Healthy fats: **4**

# PORTUGUESE CHICKEN AND EGGPLANT WITH SLAW

8 G CARB PER SERVE

ONLY 6 INGREDIENTS

🍴 **Serves 4**    🕐 **Preparation: 15 minutes**
🍲 **Cooking: 10 minutes**    👨‍🍳 **Difficulty: Low**

600 g lean chicken breast, diced
2 tablespoons olive oil
2 tablespoons Portuguese
  chicken seasoning
2 eggplants, cut into wedges
1 x 200 g packet classic coleslaw
½ cup (125 g) whole-egg mayonnaise

Preheat a barbecue chargrill plate to high.

Combine the chicken, oil, seasoning and eggplant in a bowl. Add to the chargrill plate and cook, turning occasionally, for 6 minutes or until golden and the chicken is cooked through. Transfer to serving plates.

Meanwhile, mix together the coleslaw and mayonnaise, adding a little water to loosen the mixture if needed. Season with freshly ground black pepper.

Serve the chicken and eggplant with the slaw mixture on top.

# CHICKEN PUTTANESCA

**UNITS PER SERVE**

Lean meat, fish, poultry, eggs, tofu: **1.5**
Breads, cereals, legumes, starchy
 vegetables: **0**
Dairy and dairy alternatives: **0**
Low–moderate carb vegetables: **3**
Healthy fats: **2**

🍴 **Serves 4**  🕐 **Preparation: 20 minutes**
🍲 **Cooking: 15 minutes**  👨‍🍳 **Difficulty: Low**

1 tablespoon olive oil
600 g lean chicken breast strips,
 seasoned with pepper
1 x 410 g tin rich and thick garlic
 and basil chopped tomatoes
60 g sliced black olives
1 tablespoon drained, rinsed
 baby capers in brine
large pinch dried chilli flakes
1 cup small basil leaves
2 carrots, spiralised
2 x 250 g packets fresh
 zucchini spaghetti

Heat the oil in a large, deep non-stick frying pan over high heat. Add the chicken and cook, stirring occasionally, for 5 minutes.

Reduce the heat to medium. Add the tomatoes, olives, capers, chilli and ½ cup (125 ml) water to the pan and simmer, stirring occasionally, for 10 minutes or until thickened. Stir in the basil.

Divide the carrot and zucchini among serving bowls, spoon over the chicken mixture and serve.

*fuss-free entertaining*

Lean meat, fish, poultry, eggs, tofu: **1.5**
Breads, cereals, legumes, starchy
   vegetables: **0**
Dairy and dairy alternatives: **0.5**
Low–moderate carb vegetables: **1**
Healthy fats: **2.5**

# HARISSA SALMON WITH LEMON YOGHURT

🍽 **Serves 4**   🕐 **Preparation: 15 minutes**
🍲 **Cooking: 10 minutes**   🎩 **Difficulty: Low**

2 tablespoons sunflower oil
2 teaspoons harissa paste
4 x 150 g skinless, boneless
   salmon fillets
finely grated zest and juice of 1 lemon,
   plus extra wedges to serve
200 g reduced-fat natural yoghurt
2 x 150 g bags mixed leaf kale leaf
   and spinach

Mix together the oil and harissa paste and rub over the salmon to evenly coat on all sides.

Preheat a large non-stick frying pan over medium–high heat. Add the salmon and cook for 3 minutes each side or until golden and cooked to medium. Transfer to a plate.

Whisk together the lemon zest, lemon juice and yoghurt in a jug. Season with freshly ground black pepper.

Divide the salad leaves among plates and top with the salmon. Spoon over the lemon yoghurt and serve.

Lean meat, fish, poultry, eggs, tofu: **1.5**
Breads, cereals, legumes, starchy
   vegetables: **0**
Dairy and dairy alternatives: **1**
Low–moderate carb vegetables: **2.5**
Healthy fats: **4**

# RICOTTA-STUFFED CHICKEN WITH VEGETABLE MEDLEY

🍴 **Serves 4**    🕐 **Preparation: 25 minutes**
♨ **Cooking: 20 minutes**    👳 **Difficulty: Medium**

4 x 150 g lean chicken breast fillets,
   butterflied, flattened and seasoned
   with pepper
220 g reduced-fat fresh ricotta
⅓ cup (80 g) fresh basil pesto
2 x 200 g punnets cherry tomatoes
1 x 500 g packet frozen
   broad beans, shelled
2 bunches thin asparagus, trimmed

Lay each piece of chicken out flat on a clean surface and spread one half of each piece with the ricotta. Using 1 tablespoon of the pesto, drizzle a little over the ricotta, then season with freshly ground black pepper. Fold over the chicken to enclose the filling, using toothpicks to secure.

Heat a large non-stick frying pan over medium heat. Add the chicken and cook, turning occasionally, for 15 minutes or until golden and cooked through. Transfer to a board.

Increase the heat to high. Add the tomatoes, broad beans, asparagus and ⅓ cup (80 ml) water to the pan and cook, tossing, for 3 minutes or until the vegetables are just tender and the water has evaporated. Divide among serving plates.

Slice the chicken, then place alongside the vegetables. Drizzle over the remaining pesto and serve.

Lean meat, fish, poultry, eggs, tofu: **1.5**
Breads, cereals, legumes, starchy
  vegetables: **0**
Dairy and dairy alternatives: **0**
Low–moderate carb vegetables: **2**
Healthy fats: **2**

# GREEK LAMB AND EGGPLANT WRAPS

🍴 **Serves 4**   🕐 **Preparation: 25 minutes**
♨ **Cooking: 10 minutes**   🎖 **Difficulty: Medium**

600 g lean lamb backstrap, cut into
  2 cm cubes
2 teaspoons onion, garlic and Italian
  herb paste
½ cup (125 ml) fat-free
  Greek salad dressing
2 large eggplants, thinly
  sliced lengthways
2 bunches English spinach,
  leaves picked
80 g walnuts, toasted and chopped

Preheat a barbecue flat plate and chargrill plate to high.

Combine the lamb, paste and one-third of the dressing in a bowl and season with freshly ground black pepper. Thread the lamb onto eight large metal skewers.

Mix together the eggplant and half the remaining dressing and season with freshly ground black pepper.

Add the lamb skewers and eggplant to the chargrill plate and cook, turning occasionally, for 8 minutes or until golden and the lamb is cooked to medium–well done. Transfer to a serving platter.

Cook the spinach on the barbecue flat plate for 1–2 minutes or until just wilted. Transfer to the platter, drizzle over the remaining dressing and season with freshly ground black pepper. Sprinkle the walnuts over the top and serve.

# BARBECUED BEEF WITH CHIMICHURRI PICKLED VEGETABLES

🍴 **Serves 4**   🕐 **Preparation: 15 minutes**
🍲 **Cooking: 10 minutes**   🍶 **Difficulty: Low**

2 tablespoons sunflower oil

1 tablespoon sweet paprika

600 g lean beef minute steaks, seasoned with pepper

2 eggplants, cut into wedges

500 g cauliflower florets, halved

**CHIMICHURRI PICKLED VEGETABLES**

1 tablespoon extra virgin olive oil

⅓ cup finely chopped flat-leaf parsley

⅓ cup finely chopped coriander

½ cup (125 ml) red wine vinegar

½ teaspoon dried chilli flakes (or to taste)

500 g cherry tomatoes, quartered

200 g baby button mushrooms, quartered

To make the chimichurri pickled vegetables, combine all the ingredients in a bowl and season with freshly ground black pepper. Set aside, stirring occasionally.

Preheat a barbecue chargrill plate to high.

Combine the oil, paprika and beef and set aside.

Place the eggplant and cauliflower on the chargrill plate and cook, turning occasionally, for 5 minutes or until golden and just tender. Transfer to a serving platter.

Chargrill the beef for 30 seconds each side, then add to the platter. Spoon over the chimichurri pickled vegetables and serve.

UNITS PER SERVE

Lean meat, fish, poultry, eggs, tofu: **1.5**

Breads, cereals, legumes, starchy vegetables: **0**

Dairy and dairy alternatives: **0**

Low–moderate carb vegetables: **3**

Healthy fats: **1**

# PERI PERI CHICKEN WITH GRILLED CAPSICUM RICE

**10 G CARB PER SERVE**

🍴 **Serves 4**  🕐 **Preparation: 20 minutes**
🍳 **Cooking: 20 minutes**  👨‍🍳 **Difficulty: Low**

COOKS IN **UNDER 20 MINS**

600 g small lean chicken breast fillets, each cut horizontally into 3 thin slices

2 tablespoons peri peri medium seasoning rub

1 baby cos lettuce, leaves separated

small coriander sprigs and lime wedges, to serve

### GRILLED CAPSICUM RICE

1 tablespoon olive oil

2 teaspoons smoked paprika

1 teaspoon ground cumin

1 teaspoon fresh garlic paste

1 x 400 g tin whole peeled tomatoes

1 x 500 g packet frozen broccoli and cauliflower rice

1 small red capsicum, seeded and thinly sliced

1 small green capsicum, seeded and thinly sliced

1 small red onion, cut into thin wedges

Preheat a barbecue chargrill plate to high.

To make the grilled capsicum rice, heat the oil in a large non-stick frying pan over high heat. Add the paprika, cumin, garlic paste and tomatoes and cook, stirring occasionally, for 10 minutes or until thickened and deep red in colour. Add the broccoli and cauliflower rice and cook, tossing, for 2 minutes or until heated through.

While the rice mixture is cooking, add the red and green capsicum and onion to the chargrill plate and cook for 10 minutes or until charred and tender. Stir into the rice mixture, adding a little water to loosen if needed. Season with freshly ground pepper.

Meanwhile, combine the chicken and peri peri seasoning. Add to the chargrill plate and cook, turning occasionally, for 10 minutes or until deep golden and cooked through. Transfer to a plate.

Spoon the grilled capsicum rice onto a platter and top with the chicken. Place the lettuce leaves alongside, sprinkle with the coriander sprigs and serve with the lime wedges.

**4 G CARB PER SERVE**

# CAJUN PRAWNS WITH AVOCADO PESTO

🍴 **Serves 4**   🕐 **Preparation: 15 minutes**
♨ **Cooking: 5 minutes**   🍲 **Difficulty: Low**

**COOKS IN UNDER 5 MINS**

**UNITS PER SERVE**

Lean meat, fish, poultry, eggs, tofu: **1.5**
Breads, cereals, legumes, starchy
   vegetables: **0**
Dairy and dairy alternatives: **0**
Low–moderate carb vegetables: **1**
Healthy fats: **2**

---

1 tablespoon sunflower oil
600 g peeled and deveined raw prawns
2 teaspoons Cajun seasoning
2 bunches thin asparagus, trimmed
50 g baby rocket leaves
1 bunch baby radishes, trimmed and
   very thinly sliced into rounds

**AVOCADO PESTO**

80 g avocado
¼ cup coriander leaves
¼ cup basil leaves
⅓ cup (80 ml) red wine vinegar

To make the avocado pesto, place all the ingredients in a blender or food processor and blend until smooth, adding a little water to loosen if needed. Season with freshly ground black pepper.

Heat the oil in a large non-stick frying pan over high heat. Add the prawns and Cajun seasoning and cook, tossing, for 3 minutes or until golden and cooked. Transfer to a plate. Add the asparagus to the pan and cook, tossing, for 1 minute or until bright green and just tender.

Divide the rocket, radish, asparagus and prawns among plates and serve with the avocado pesto.

# SEAFOOD WITH CHILLI OIL AND PEA PUREE

🍴 **Serves 4**   🕐 **Preparation: 15 minutes**
♨ **Cooking: 15 minutes**   ⑤ **Difficulty: Medium**

2 spring onions, white and
   green parts sliced

2 teaspoons ground coriander

2 cups (300 g) frozen peas

2 zucchini, chopped

600 g fresh marinara mix
   (prawns, mussels, white fish,
   salmon and squid)

2 cups mixed salad leaves (curly endive,
   green oak, red witlof, baby herbs)

lime wedges, to serve

**CHILLI OIL**

⅓ cup (80 ml) sunflower oil

2 long red chillies, chopped

2 cm piece ginger, finely chopped

2 cloves garlic, finely chopped

½ cup small coriander leaves

Combine the spring onion, ground coriander, peas, zucchini and ½ cup (125 ml) water in a saucepan over high heat. Cook, covered and stirring occasionally, for 10 minutes or until the vegetables are soft and the water has evaporated. Transfer the mixture to an upright blender and blend until completely smooth, adding a little extra water if needed to loosen. Cover to keep warm.

Meanwhile, to make the chilli oil, place all the ingredients in a large non-stick frying pan over medium heat. Cook, stirring, for 5 minutes until light golden and crisp. Transfer the hot oil to a heatproof jug.

Reheat the pan over high heat. Add the marinara mix and cook, tossing constantly, for 3 minutes or until the seafood is just cooked. Season with freshly ground black pepper.

Spoon the pea puree into the centre of serving plates and top with the seafood. Drizzle over the chilli oil and serve.

# ROAST LAMB WITH PARSLEY PINE NUT DRESSING

**UNITS PER SERVE**

Lean meat, fish, poultry, eggs, tofu: **1.5**
Breads, cereals, legumes, starchy
vegetables: **0**
Dairy and dairy alternatives: **0**
Low–moderate carb vegetables: **3**
Healthy fats: **4**

🍽 **Serves 4**    🕐 **Preparation: 20 minutes**
♨ **Cooking: 20 minutes**    👨‍🍳 **Difficulty: Low**

600 g lean lamb fillets,
   seasoned with pepper
4 zucchini, cut lengthways into quarters
300 g peeled, seeded pumpkin,
   cut into thin wedges
2 bunches asparagus, trimmed
2 tablespoons olive oil
1 tablespoon cumin seeds
⅓ cup oregano leaves

**PARSLEY PINE NUT DRESSING**

1 small bunch flat-leaf parsley, chopped
1 long green chilli, chopped
2 spring onions, white and green
   parts chopped
½ cup (125 ml) red wine vinegar
80 g pine nuts, toasted

Preheat the oven to 220°C (200°C fan-forced). Line a large baking tray with baking paper.

Place the lamb, zucchini, pumpkin, asparagus, oil, cumin seeds and oregano in a bowl and mix together well. Season with freshly ground black pepper. Spread evenly over the prepared tray and roast for 20 minutes or until golden and the lamb is cooked to medium–well done.

Meanwhile, to make the parsley pine nut dressing, combine all the ingredients in a jug and season with freshly ground black pepper.

Remove the lamb and place on a board. Transfer the vegetables to serving plates. Slice the lamb, then place on top of the vegetables. Drizzle with the parsley pine nut dressing and serve.

Lean meat, fish, poultry, eggs, tofu: **1.5**
Breads, cereals, legumes, starchy
   vegetables: **0**
Dairy and dairy alternatives: **0**
Low–moderate carb vegetables: **2.5**
Healthy fats: **4**

# CHICKEN ZOODLE LETTUCE CUPS

🍴 Serves 4    🕐 Preparation: 15 minutes
〰️ Cooking: 10 minutes    👨‍🍳 Difficulty: Low

600 g lean chicken breast fillet, diced
   and seasoned with pepper
¼ cup (60 g) fresh Thai herb paste
1 red onion, cut into thin wedges
2 x 250 g packets fresh
   zucchini spaghetti
juice of 1 lemon, plus
   extra wedges to serve
8 large iceberg lettuce cups

Heat a large non-stick wok over high heat. Add the chicken, herb paste and onion and stir-fry for 5 minutes or until the chicken is cooked.

Add the zucchini and 2 tablespoons water and stir-fry for 1 minute to heat through. Remove the wok from the heat and toss through the lemon juice.

Arrange the lettuce cups on serving plates. Spoon the chicken mixture evenly into the cups and serve.

# CRUMBED LAMB CUTLETS WITH MINTY PEA MIX

**10 G CARB PER SERVE**

🍴 **Serves 4**     🕐 **Preparation: 25 minutes**
♨ **Cooking: 20 minutes**     👐 **Difficulty: Medium**

**UNITS PER SERVE**

Lean meat, fish, poultry, eggs, tofu: **1.5**

Breads, cereals, legumes, starchy
vegetables: **0**

Dairy and dairy alternatives: **0**

Low–moderate carb vegetables: **2**

Healthy fats: **4**

---

1 x 55 g egg

80 g almond meal

1 long red chilli, finely chopped

2 cloves garlic, finely chopped

2 tablespoons finely chopped chives

550 g extra-trim Frenched lamb cutlets,
seasoned with pepper

2 tablespoons olive oil

**MINTY PEA MIX**

1½ cups (225 g) frozen baby peas

200 g sugar snap peas

500 g broccoli florets

½ cup (125 ml) salt-reduced
chicken stock

finely grated zest and juice of 1 lemon

1 cup small mint leaves

---

Line a large baking tray with baking paper. Crack the egg into a bowl and lightly beat, then season with freshly ground black pepper. Combine the almond meal, chilli, garlic and chives in a separate bowl and season with freshly ground black pepper. Working with one at a time, brush the egg over both sides of each lamb cutlet, then sprinkle with the almond meal mixture to lightly coat. Transfer to the prepared tray and place in the fridge to chill.

To make the minty pea mix, combine the baby peas, sugar snaps, broccoli and stock in a saucepan over high heat and bring to the boil. Boil, partially covered and stirring occasionally, for 8 minutes or until just tender and the stock has reduced completely. Remove the pan from the heat and stir in the lemon zest, lemon juice and mint. Season with freshly ground black pepper, then cover to keep warm.

Heat the oil in a large non-stick frying pan over high heat. Add half the lamb cutlets and cook, turning occasionally, for 5 minutes or until golden and cooked to medium. Transfer to a plate and cover, then repeat with the remaining cutlets.

Scoop the minty pea mix onto serving plates, top with the lamb cutlets and serve.

# CHICKEN PICCATA

**UNITS PER SERVE**

Lean meat, fish, poultry, eggs, tofu: **1.5**

Breads, cereals, legumes, starchy
   vegetables: **0**

Dairy and dairy alternatives: **0.5**

Low–moderate carb vegetables: **2**

Healthy fats: **2**

🍴 Serves 4    🕐 Preparation: 20 minutes
🍲 Cooking: 20 minutes    👐 Difficulty: Low

8 G CARB PER SERVE

**COOKS IN UNDER 20 MINS**

2 tablespoons olive oil

600 g small lean chicken breast fillets,
   each sliced in half horizontally

1 onion, halved and thinly sliced

3 cloves garlic, thinly sliced

1 tablespoon drained, rinsed
   baby capers in brine

1 cup (250 ml) salt-reduced
   chicken stock

300 g baby green beans, trimmed

200 g reduced-fat natural yoghurt

2 tablespoons thyme leaves

300 g mixed salad leaves (red
   radicchio, baby rocket, baby cos),
   dressed with lemon juice

Heat 1 tablespoon oil in a large, deep non-stick frying pan over
high heat. Add half the chicken and cook, turning occasionally,
for 2 minutes or until golden on all sides. Transfer to a plate and
repeat with the remaining chicken.

Reduce the heat to medium and heat the remaining oil in the pan.
Add the onion and cook, stirring, for 5 minutes or until golden and
softened. Return the chicken to the pan and add the garlic, capers
and stock. Bring to a rapid simmer, stirring, then cook, turning the
chicken occasionally, for 2 minutes. Add the beans and simmer,
turning occasionally, for 6 minutes or until the beans are tender,
the chicken is cooked and the sauce has reduced by two-thirds.
Remove the pan from the heat and stand for 2 minutes.

Add the yoghurt and thyme to the pan and stir to combine. Season
with freshly ground black pepper. Take to the table in the pan and
serve with the dressed salad leaves.

600 g thick piece lean beef fillet,
 seasoned with pepper
2 bunches broccolini, trimmed
 and halved lengthways
2 bunches English spinach,
 leaves picked
1 tablespoon extra virgin olive oil
small basil leaves, to serve

**SALSA ROSSA**

1 tablespoon extra virgin olive oil
1 teaspoon fresh garlic paste
2 large pinches dried chilli flakes
1 x 400 g tin whole peeled tomatoes
⅓ cup (80 ml) red wine vinegar

# SEARED BEEF WITH SALSA ROSSA

6 G
CARB PER
SERVE

🍽 Serves 4    🕐 Preparation: 25 minutes
🍳 Cooking: 20 minutes    👨‍🍳 Difficulty: Medium

COOKS IN **UNDER 20 MINS**

Heat a large non-stick frying pan over medium–high heat. Add the beef and cook, turning occasionally, for 15–18 minutes or until golden and cooked to medium–rare.

Meanwhile, to make the salsa rossa, place all the ingredients in a saucepan over medium–low heat and cook, stirring occasionally, for 15 minutes until the sauce reduces and thickens, and becomes a rich red colour. Season with freshly ground black pepper.

Transfer the beef to a board. Reheat the frying pan over high heat, add the broccolini, spinach and ⅓ cup (80 ml) water and cook, tossing, for 3 minutes or until the broccolini is just tender and the spinach has wilted. Season with freshly ground black pepper.

Spoon the salsa rossa over a platter and top with the vegetables. Thinly slice the beef, then layer over the top and drizzle with the extra virgin olive oil. Season with freshly ground black pepper, sprinkle with the basil and serve.

Lean meat, fish, poultry, eggs, tofu: **1.5**
Breads, cereals, legumes, starchy
   vegetables: **0**
Dairy and dairy alternatives: **0**
Low–moderate carb vegetables: **1.5**
Healthy fats: **0**

# SOY BAKED FISH PARCELS

10 G CARB PER SERVE

ONLY **6** INGREDIENTS

🍽 **Serves 4**   🕐 **Preparation: 20 minutes**
▒ **Cooking: 15 minutes**   🖐 **Difficulty: Medium**

2 x 250 g packets fresh
   zucchini spaghetti
1 x 450 g packet frozen steam fresh
   beans, broccoli and sugar snap peas
4 x 150 g thick-cut skinless,
   boneless barramundi fillets,
   seasoned with pepper
¼ cup (60 ml) salt-reduced soy sauce
1 teaspoon sesame oil
5 cm piece ginger, cut into
   thin matchsticks

Preheat the oven to 220°C (200°C fan-forced). Place four large pieces of foil on a work surface, then cover each with a piece of baking paper.

Place the zucchini in the centre of each piece of paper. Top with the frozen vegetables, then the fish, soy sauce, oil and ginger. Season with freshly ground black pepper, then fold up the edges to firmly enclose the filling.

Place the parcels directly on the oven shelves and bake for 15 minutes. Transfer to serving plates and take to the table, allowing your guests to open their own parcels.

Lean meat, fish, poultry, eggs, tofu: **1.5**

Breads, cereals, legumes, starchy vegetables: **0**

Dairy and dairy alternatives: **0**

Low–moderate carb vegetables: **1.5**

Healthy fats: **0**

# STEAK AND MUSTARD SAUCE WITH BROCCOLI AND PEA MASH

7 G CARB PER SERVE

ONLY **6** INGREDIENTS

🍴 Serves 4    🕐 Preparation: 15 minutes

🍳 Cooking: 20 minutes    🍲 Difficulty: Low

500 g broccoli florets

1¼ cups (180 g) frozen baby peas

1 cup (250 ml) salt-reduced beef stock

4 x 150 g beef eye fillet steaks, seasoned with pepper

2 tablespoons Dijon mustard

1 x 140 g bag chopped kale

Place the broccoli, peas and half the stock in a large, deep non-stick frying pan over high heat. Bring to the boil and cook, stirring occasionally, for 8 minutes or until just tender and the stock has evaporated. Transfer the mixture to a large bowl and season with freshly ground black pepper, then cover and set aside.

Reheat the pan over high heat. Add the beef and cook for 3 minutes each side or until golden and cooked to medium–rare. Transfer to a plate. Add the mustard, kale and remaining stock to the pan and stir to scrape any flavourings off the base. Cook, stirring, for 3 minutes or until the kale has wilted and the sauce has reduced by one-third and thickened slightly.

Roughly mash the broccoli mixture, then divide among serving plates. Top with the steaks, spoon over the kale and mustard sauce and serve.

# FENNEL PORK WITH BEETROOT CEVICHE

**UNITS PER SERVE**

Lean meat, fish, poultry, eggs, tofu: **1.5**
Breads, cereals, legumes, starchy
    vegetables: **0**
Dairy and dairy alternatives: **1**
Low–moderate carb vegetables: **3**
Healthy fats: **2**

Serves 4    Preparation: 20 minutes
Cooking: 20 minutes    Difficulty: Medium

2 tablespoons fennel seeds
1 teaspoon cayenne pepper
600 g lean pork medallions,
    seasoned with pepper
2 tablespoons olive oil
1 leek, white part only,
    thinly sliced into rounds
2 small bulbs baby fennel, trimmed
    and thinly sliced lengthways,
    fronds reserved
2 bunches English spinach,
    leaves trimmed
80 g reduced-fat feta, crumbled

**BEETROOT CEVICHE**

150 g peeled beetroot, coarsely grated
1 small clove garlic, crushed
finely grated zest and juice of 2 lemons
1 cup coriander leaves

To make the beetroot ceviche, combine all the ingredients in a bowl and season with ½ teaspoon freshly ground black pepper. Set aside, turning occasionally.

Sprinkle the fennel seeds and cayenne pepper evenly over the pork, coating well on all sides. Heat the oil in a large non-stick frying pan over high heat, add the pork and cook for 4 minutes each side or until golden and just cooked. Transfer to a plate.

Reheat the pan over high heat. Add the leek, sliced fennel and ⅓ cup (80 ml) water and cook, tossing, for 5 minutes or until starting to soften. Add the spinach and cook, covered and tossing occasionally, for 3 minutes or until the spinach has wilted and the leek and fennel are tender.

Divide the vegetables among serving plates and top with the pork. Spoon over the beetroot ceviche, then sprinkle with the feta and fennel fronds and serve.

# SUMAC BEEF AND ZUCCHINI MINT SALAD

🍴 Serves 4    🕐 Preparation: 15 minutes

♨ Cooking: 10 minutes    👨‍🍳 Difficulty: Low

2 tablespoons olive oil

600 g trimmed beef topside

1 tablespoon sumac

500 g small tomatoes

**ZUCCHINI MINT SALAD**

4 zucchini, thinly sliced into rounds

⅓ cup (80 ml) white wine vinegar

2 spring onions, white and green
parts thinly sliced

1 cup small mint leaves

80 g reduced-fat feta, crumbled

Preheat a barbecue chargrill plate to high.

To make the zucchini mint salad, mix together all the ingredients in a bowl and season with freshly ground black pepper. Set aside, tossing occasionally.

Combine the oil, beef and sumac in a bowl and season with freshly ground black pepper. Add the beef mixture and tomatoes to the chargrill plate and cook, turning occasionally, for 8 minutes or until the meat is cooked to medium. Transfer the beef to a board, and the tomatoes to a plate.

Arrange the zucchini salad on a platter. Slice the beef and place on top, then scatter with the tomatoes and serve.

## DETERMINING YOUR DAILY KILOJOULE REQUIREMENTS

The following calculation was used in our scientific trial to personalise the diet to each participant's energy needs. It estimates your daily kilojoule requirements to maintain normal body function and keep your weight stable. This is known as your basal metabolic rate (BMR). To determine your BMR, use the appropriate formula from the table below.

**Formulas for calculating your basal metabolic rate** →

| Age (years) | BMR equation | |
| --- | --- | --- |
| | Women | Men |
| 18–29 | (62 x weight in kilograms) + 2036 | (63 x weight in kilograms) + 2896 |
| 30–59 | (34 x weight in kilograms) + 3538 | (48 x weight in kilograms) + 3653 |
| 60 and over | (38 x weight in kilograms) + 2755 | (49 x weight in kilograms) + 2459 |

Note: There are a few different methods for calculating BMR. We've used the Schofield equation.

Once you've determined your BMR, you need to multiply it by an activity factor from the table below to estimate your total daily kilojoule requirements.

**Activity factors for determining your total daily kilojoule requirements** →

| Activity level | Description | Activity factor | |
| --- | --- | --- | --- |
| | | Women | Men |
| Sedentary | Very physically inactive (work and leisure) | 1.3 | 1.3 |
| Lightly active | Daily activity of walking or intense exercise once or twice a week and a sedentary job | 1.5 | 1.6 |
| Moderately active | Intense exercise lasting 20–45 minutes at least three times a week or an active job with a lot of daily walking | 1.6 | 1.7 |
| Very active | Intense exercise lasting at least one hour each day or a heavy, physical job | 1.9 | 2.1 |
| Extremely active | Daily intense activity (i.e. nonstop training, e.g. an athlete in training) or a highly demanding physical job (e.g. armed forces) | 2.2 | 2.4 |

If you're a healthy weight, there's no need to reduce your energy intake, so the number you're left with now is your daily requirement, and you can use this to choose the level from the table on page 26.

If you need to lose weight, calculate your daily kilojoule requirement as follows. To reduce your weight by about 0.5 kilogram each week, you'll need to reduce your energy intake by 2000 kJ per day. Once you've calculated your total daily kilojoule requirements above, subtract 2000 from this number to determine how many kilojoules to eat each day to achieve weight loss, and therefore which of the four levels to choose.

To reduce your weight by about 1 kilogram each week, you'll need to reduce your energy intake by 4000 kJ per day. Calculate your total daily kilojoule needs as above and subtract 4000. This will tell you how many kilojoules to eat each day to achieve this weight loss and therefore which of the four levels to choose.

## HOW IT WORKS IN PRACTICE

Sylvia is 58 years old and weighs 87 kilograms. She works part time as an office assistant and looks after her grandchildren two days a week. Sylvia goes for a walk most days. This makes her activity factor 1.5. She chooses the appropriate formula from the table opposite and calculates her BMR like this:

> BMR = (34 x weight in kilograms) + 3538
> = (34 x 87) + 3538
> = 6496 kJ per day

To calculate her total daily kilojoule requirements, Sylvia will multiply her BMR by her activity factor:

> Total daily energy requirement = 6496 x 1.5
> = 9744 kJ per day

This is the amount of energy Sylvia needs to maintain her current weight.

Sylvia is overweight and would like to start by losing about 0.5 kilogram a week. She'll therefore reduce her estimated total daily kilojoule intake by 2000 kJ per day:

> Total dieting energy requirement = 9744 – 2000
> = 7744 kJ per day

Sylvia rounds this down to the nearest thousand, 7000 kJ per day, and will therefore start on level 2. If she's feeling too hungry or losing weight too rapidly, Sylvia can move to level 3 (8000 kJ). If she's not losing weight, she can drop down to level 1 (6000 kJ).

**Our clinical experience has shown that if your calculated energy requirements are greater than 9000 kJ a day, even by 2000–3000 kJ, following the level 4 diet will still result in significant health benefits.**

### Maintenance in the longer term

Sylvia reaches her weight-loss goal after six weeks, and her health has improved significantly. She decides she's enjoying the diet but would like to eat some fruit each day. As she's now on maintenance, she can have up to 70 grams carbohydrates each day, instead of the standard 50 grams. To add another carbohydrate serve, she uses the carbohydrate extras table on page 25 to select a fruit portion.

## See how you progress

If your chosen level isn't working, you can move between levels until you start to see the changes you desire. Many people hit a weight-loss plateau after an initial drop in weight. If this happens, you can simply switch to a lower level until you reach your target. Your dietitian and exercise physiologist can also help you overcome a weight plateau.

# Notes

**Page 19** In fact, a recent study comparing the effects of diets with different levels of carbohydrate...: Harvey CJDC, Schofield GM, Zinn C, Thornley SJ, Crofts C, Merien FLR., 'Low-carbohydrate diets differing in carbohydrate restriction improve cardiometabolic and anthropometric markers in healthy adults: A randomised clinical trial', PeerJ 2019, Feb 5;7:e6273. doi: 10.7717/peerj.6273.

**Page 21** Across 12 different studies of almost 1000 patients with type 2 diabetes...: Suyoto PST, 'Effect of low-carbohydrate diet on markers of renal function in patients with type 2 diabetes: A meta-analysis', *Diabetes Metabolism Research and Reviews* 2018, vol. 34, no. 7, e3032. doi: 10.1002/dmrr.3032.

**Page 22** A 2018 study also showed that in people with type 2 diabetes...: Myette-Côté É, Durrer C, Neudorf H, Bammert TD, Botezelli JD, Johnson JD, DeSouza CA, Little JP, 'The effect of a short-term low-carbohydrate, high-fat diet with or without postmeal walks on glycemic control and inflammation in type 2 diabetes: a randomized trial', *American Journal of Physiology Regulatory Integrative and Comparitive Physiology* 2018, vol. 315, no. 6, pp. R1210–R9. doi: 10.1152/ajpregu.00240.2018.

# Recipe conversion chart

Measuring cups and spoons may vary slightly from one country to another, but the difference is generally not enough to affect a recipe. All cup and spoon measures are level.

One Australian metric measuring cup holds 250 ml (8 fl oz), one Australian tablespoon holds 20 ml (4 teaspoons) and one Australian metric teaspoon holds 5 ml. North America, New Zealand and the UK use a 15 ml (3-teaspoon) tablespoon.

## LENGTH

| METRIC | IMPERIAL |
|---|---|
| 3 mm | ⅛ inch |
| 6 mm | ¼ inch |
| 1 cm | ½ inch |
| 2.5 cm | 1 inch |
| 5 cm | 2 inches |
| 18 cm | 7 inches |
| 20 cm | 8 inches |
| 23 cm | 9 inches |
| 25 cm | 10 inches |
| 30 cm | 12 inches |

## LIQUID MEASURES

| ONE AMERICAN PINT | ONE IMPERIAL PINT |
|---|---|
| 500 ml (16 fl oz) | 600 ml (20 fl oz) |

| CUP | METRIC | IMPERIAL |
|---|---|---|
| ⅛ cup | 30 ml | 1 fl oz |
| ¼ cup | 60 ml | 2 fl oz |
| ⅓ cup | 80 ml | 2½ fl oz |
| ½ cup | 125 ml | 4 fl oz |
| ⅔ cup | 160 ml | 5 fl oz |
| ¾ cup | 180 ml | 6 fl oz |
| 1 cup | 250 ml | 8 fl oz |
| 2 cups | 500 ml | 16 fl oz |
| 2¼ cups | 560 ml | 20 fl oz |
| 4 cups | 1 litre | 32 fl oz |

## DRY MEASURES

The most accurate way to measure dry ingredients is to weigh them. However, if using a cup, add the ingredient loosely to the cup and level with a knife; don't compact the ingredient unless the recipe requests 'firmly packed'.

| METRIC | IMPERIAL |
|---|---|
| 15 g | ½ oz |
| 30 g | 1 oz |
| 60 g | 2 oz |
| 125 g | 4 oz (¼ lb) |
| 185 g | 6 oz |
| 250 g | 8 oz (½ lb) |
| 375 g | 12 oz (¾ lb) |
| 500 g | 16 oz (1 lb) |
| 1 kg | 32 oz (2 lb) |

## OVEN TEMPERATURES

| CELSIUS | FAHRENHEIT | CELSIUS | GAS MARK |
|---|---|---|---|
| 100°C | 200°F | 110°C | ¼ |
| 120°C | 250°F | 130°C | ½ |
| 150°C | 300°F | 140°C | 1 |
| 160°C | 325°F | 150°C | 2 |
| 180°C | 350°F | 170°C | 3 |
| 200°C | 400°F | 180°C | 4 |
| 220°C | 425°F | 190°C | 5 |
| | | 200°C | 6 |
| | | 220°C | 7 |
| | | 230°C | 8 |
| | | 240°C | 9 |
| | | 250°C | 10 |

# Acknowledgements

First, we'd like to thank the contributors to *The CSIRO Low-Carb Diet* and *CSIRO Low-Carb Every Day* books. To Dr Natalie Luscombe-Marsh (CSIRO), Dr Tom Wycherley (University of South Australia), Professor Campbell Thompson (University of Adelaide) and Professor Manny Noakes (formerly of CSIRO), thank you for your knowledge, expertise, guidance and tireless contribution to the research underpinning the scientific evidence supporting the CSIRO low-carb diet lifestyle plan; to Megan Rebuli (CSIRO) for revision of the recipes and menu design. To Dr Gilly Hendrie (CSIRO) and Danielle Baird (CSIRO) for your review of the environmental sustainability of the CSIRO low-carb diet. Collectively, your contribution to the information presented in these publications has been invaluable to their incredible success.

We also express our deep thanks to our scientific co-investigators and collaborators for their contributions to our scientific ideas and their guidance and commitment to this important research topic: Dr Jeannie Tay (CSIRO and Agency for Science Technology and Research, Singapore); Professor Jon Buckley (University of South Australia); Professor Gary Wittert (University of Adelaide); Associate Professor William Yancy Jr (Duke University, USA); Professor Carlene Wilson (Flinders University, South Australia); Dr Vanessa Danthiir (CSIRO); Dr Ian Zajac (CSIRO) and Professor Peter Clifton (University of South Australia).

We thank the following individuals at the Clinical Research Team at CSIRO Health and Biosecurity in South Australia for their tireless work in conducting the clinical research activities that underpin the contents of this book: Anne McGuffin, Julia Weaver and Vanessa Courage for coordinating the research trials; Janna Lutze, Dr Paul Foster, Xenia Cleantheous, Gemma Williams,

Hannah Gilbert and Fiona Barr for assisting in designing and implementing the dietary interventions; Lindy Lawson, Theresa McKinnon, Rosemary McArthur and Heather Webb for their nursing expertise and clinical patient management; Vanessa Russell, Cathryn Pape, Candita Dang, Andre Nikolic and Sylvia Usher for performing biochemical assays and for other laboratory expertise; Julie Syrette and Kathryn Bastiaans for data management; Kylie Lange and Mary Barnes for assisting with statistical analyses; Andreas Kahl and Ofa Fitzgibbons for communications; and our external fitness partners and health coaches for implementing the exercise interventions, including Luke Johnston and Annie Hastwell of Fit for Success; Kelly French, Jason Delfos, Kristi Lacey-Powell, Marilyn Woods, John Perrin, Simon Pane and Annette Beckette of South Australian Aquatic and Leisure Centre; and Angie Mondello and Josh Gniadek of Boot Camp Plus.

Thanks to the editorial and publishing team at Pan Macmillan Australia: Ingrid Ohlsson, who supported the writing of this book with great enthusiasm and encouragement; and to Virginia Birch, Naomi Van Groll and Sarah Odgers for their tireless work and support through the editorial and design process. Thanks also to editor Katri Hilden, recipe developer Tracey Pattison, recipe editor Rachel Carter, photographer Rob Palmer, stylist Emma Knowles and home economist Peta Dent. Lastly, thanks to the wonderful Lucy Inglis for her stellar work on publicity.

Finally, and most importantly, we'd like to thank the research volunteers for their participation in our research trials. It's only through their contributions that our research and these significant advancements in clinical practices for weight and diabetes management have been made possible.

# INDEX

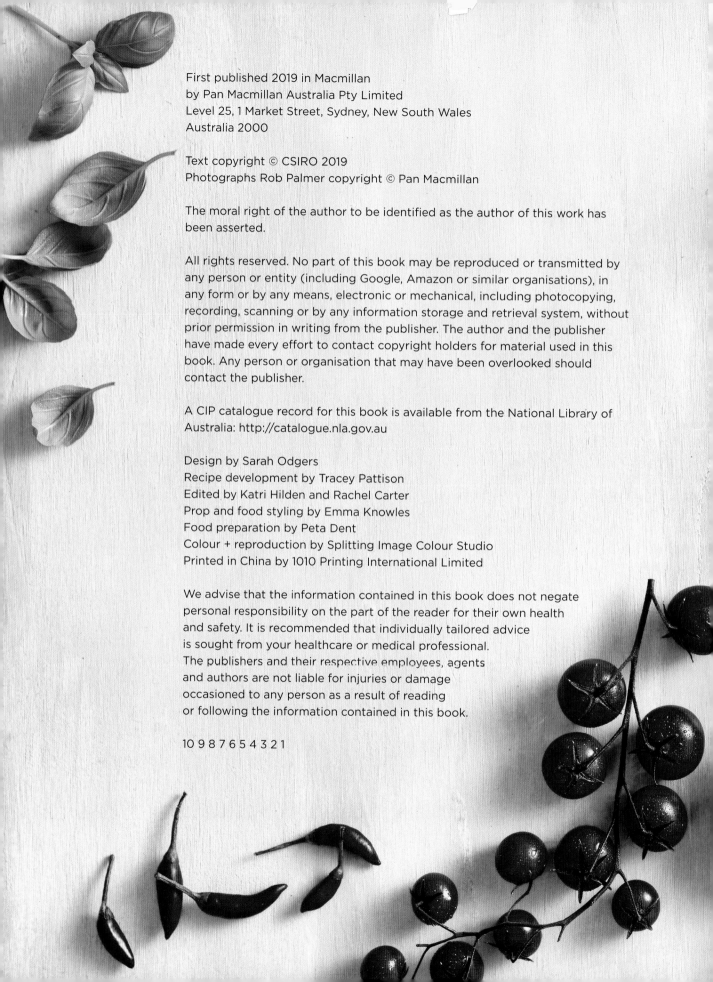

First published 2019 in Macmillan
by Pan Macmillan Australia Pty Limited
Level 25, 1 Market Street, Sydney, New South Wales
Australia 2000

A CIP catalogue record for this book is available from the National Library of
Australia: http://catalogue.nla.gov.au

Design by Sarah Odgers
Recipe development by Tracey Pattison
Edited by Katri Hilden and Rachel Carter
Prop and food styling by Emma Knowles
Food preparation by Peta Dent
Colour + reproduction by Splitting Image Colour Studio
Printed in China by 1010 Printing International Limited

10 9 8 7 6 5 4 3 2 1